BLAGDON LOC.
HISTORY SOCIETY

A History
of Blagdon

VOLUME 2

to be published as a series of journals

Adam and Eve
C15th misericord from St Andrew's Parish Church, Blagdon

December 2006

Editor - Neil Bentham

Assistant Editors - Peter King & Sheila Johnson

Typeset in Bembo
Imprint: GWP / FWB. England
Funded by a grant from the Local Heritage Initiative

ISBN 0-9548125-4-9
      978-0-9548125-4-6

Contents

Introduction

The Society's interest in all aspects of Blagdon's history continues to grow, and its archive contains, in addition to individuals' research interests, photographs, oral recordings, artefacts, business records, receipts, and certificates awarded to school children as well as adults, whose successes in flower shows or ploughing matches is notable. Most of these items have been donated to the Society and they all add to the growing mosaic that, piece by piece, gradually widens our understanding of the past.

The Society is particularly interested in all early photographs of villagers, and if there is a glimpse of buildings, trees, vehicles or distant countryside in the background so much the better. If the photo contains a person's name or date that is most valuable. The group photograph of sports team, outing or family is welcomed, especially so if names and dates are noted on the back.

This second volume of the *History of Blagdon* continues the format of volume 1, published in December 2004, by extending the research into other aspects of the village's past, spanning the last two thousand years. An appendix lists the topics that still await the interest of researchers for further volumes.

The topics are an eclectic selection of interest to the authors and, although set out in chronological order, the subject matter is separated by centuries on a historical timeline. The intention in succeeding volumes, is to attempt to fill some of the gaps.

The individual authors' approach to their subject stems from their initial interest. Some essays rely on research using primary and secondary sources, others rely on hearsay, local knowledge and memories. Each method has its strengths and obvious weaknesses, but the view has been taken that it is better to have a half-remembered tradition than nothing at all. A history such as this is never complete, since new facts, discoveries and previously unseen documents and mementos emerge from all sorts of unusual places. Whatever their origin, they will all help some future historian to correct some of the conjectures and biases that we may have inadvertently written and thus restore the balance towards the truth. The events that occupy our passing years need to be captured and set down so that our children may perhaps, in turn, learn something of their forefathers and hopefully add, in due time, their own experiences.

Volume 1 was received with much interest, and if success can be measured in sales then out of the five hundred copies printed only a handful are now left, and these are gradually being sold. However, a few copies will be retained in the Society's archive for the longer term future. Copies of volume 1 were donated to all the local public libraries, to Bristol University Library, the British Library and the Bodleian Library in Oxford. Volume 2 will be distributed in a similar manner, with each member of Blagdon Local History Society receiving a complimentary copy.

In addition to some of the committee members, the Society's thanks are due to Elizabeth Harvey for her essay on Hannah More (a second essay is forthcoming), to Tony Staveacre for the oral histories of Flo Addicott and Ikie Smart, to Andy Littlejones for The Creation of the Ecclesiastical Parish known as Blagdon with Charterhouse on Mendip, and to Siobhan Watson for her research into the Roman occupation of this area.

Independently of this research, but relevant to it, is the fact that sixteen years ago, in 1990, Dick Wood found a small coin in the churchyard. This coin has recently been examined by the staff at Taunton Museum and identified as a Roman coin bearing the head of the Emperor Constantine I (c.285-337), 'Constantine the Great', who ruled the Roman Empire from AD 306 to 337.

In 2005, the research editor for the nineteenth and twentieth centuries of the *Oxford dictionary of national biography* (DNB) wrote to us seeking further information about their entry concerning one of Blagdon's former Rectors, the Rev. Dr Daniel Guildford Wait (1789-1850). Thanks to research by Dick Wood, following an inquiry from Dr Tony Batchelor, a distant relative of the Wait family who visited St Andrew's and spoke to John Drinkwater (churchwarden), the Society has been able to contribute to the accuracy of the entry in the DNB (which was recently reissued online.)

Again I should like to thank the committee and members for all their support and continuing contribution to the work of the Society in so many ways.

My thanks are also due to Graham and Joanna Brown & Staff for sales through Blagdon Stores.

In volume 1, in addition to some small errors that escaped, one error that must be put right is in connection with the photograph by Colin Baxter Photography Ltd, and the omission of an acknowledgment to Pauline and the late John Beasley, who commissioned the photograph during their years as postmaster to the village.

The Society's thanks are due to Daphne Watts and the Maltwood Fund for their generous donation and grant towards the cost of a computer data projector. In addition we were delighted to receive a grant from the Nationwide Building Society which has enabled us to update our computer equipment, and purchase the long awaited data projector. This new equipment will allow us to present our research to the village and wider community in a more lively and informative manner.

My grateful thanks are due to Dr Peter King for his valued suggestions and contribution to proof reading also to Olga Shotton and Sheila Johnson.

As in volume 1 an appendix has been included of the lectures, events and recent history forums that have enriched our understanding of Blagdon's history over the past years.

Finally the Society's thanks are again due to Mrs Mary Mead for all her support and to the Local Heritage Initiative administrative staff for their grant that has enabled the publication of volume 2 in 2006 and the follow-on publications over the next two years or so. At the time of writing the Countryside Agency, along with the Local Heritage Initiative, has been closed down. It is appropriate to put on record the help, co-operation and support that we, and many others, have received from the administrators and staff over the past decade. They have been succeeded by the Heritage Lottery Fund (HLF), based in Exeter, and it is they who will continue the work of monitoring our progress towards the completion of this source of funding for our village history. We look forward to working with them in the same spirit in the future.

Dr Neil Bentham
Editor. BLHS, September 2006

Romano-British Settlement in the Yeo Valley, North Somerset

Siobhan Watson

1   Introduction

What was happening in and around Blagdon and the rest of the Yeo valley during the Roman occupation of Britain? Did Roman families picnic on the Mead? Did chariots clog the high street? This chapter will seek to establish how our village fits into the current picture of Roman Somerset. When we talk about the 'Romans' in Britain we need to bear in mind that most of the 'Romans' were in fact native Iron Age people, who lived and farmed the area. These locals who adopted Roman culture and Romanised ways of building and farming are referred to as 'Romano-British', as they are Romanised local British people. The Roman occupation of Britain dates from AD 43 until approximately 409. During this time the local late Iron Age tribes swapped open-plan round houses with earthen floors and central hearths for rectangular stone houses, with rooms for specific purposes, such as dining rooms, and kitchens. Roman style houses (often referred to as 'villas') were built to a standardised layout, and some of the higher status villas had under-floor heating, hot baths, plastered and painted walls, and mosaic tile floors, although this is by no means always the case. This chapter sets out to explore the evidence for Romano-British settlements in Blagdon – but to make sense of the local landscape we need to assess the Yeo valley as a whole; and to consider the relationship between sites in the Yeo valley and the Roman mining town at Charterhouse-on-Mendip.

The Yeo valley has earned the distinction of being one of the most beautiful and tranquil micro-regions in North Somerset. It is a rural valley with pastoral farming, which ensures that the green swathes of meadow remain richly diverse. Located north of the Mendip hills, it is surrounded by four geographically distinct landscapes. Two major ranges of hills border the valley to the north and south; the North Somerset levels stretch westward to the Severn Estuary and the undulating landscape of the Chew valley curves away eastward. The Mendips dominate the skyline towards the south of the Yeo valley, and rise to over 1,000 feet, with the highest areas being the heather- and bracken-covered moorland. The Mendip plateau is significantly colder and more exposed than the Yeo valley to the north. The hills are mainly composed of carboniferous limestone and triassic dolomitic conglomerate with a core of Old Red sandstone, but localised outcrops of earlier lavas and tuffs are also evident (Goudie and Gardner, 1985.) Outcrops of carboniferous limestone occur along the northern edge of Mendip (British Geological Survey. Wells Sheet, 280. Solid and Drift Edition. 1: 50,000). North of Blagdon, the hills around Nempnett and Butcombe are formed of triassic and liassic deposits presumably overlying the carboniferous rocks. These hills rise steadily from 300 to 400 ft above OD (orthometric datum, or mean sea level) immediately north-west of our area to a maximum of 664 ft at Potters Hill. The geology of Broadfield Down (on the north flank of the Yeo valley), while less dramatic than Mendip, is nonetheless one of significant height and atmospheric conditions. The weather is known to be so reliably unpleasant on Broadfield, that in the 1940s the RAF constructed a poor weather landing strip along the top of the down, for use in training pilots to land in treacherous weather conditions. Rather surprisingly, this site has now been developed into Bristol International Airport, formerly known as Lulsgate Airport. Along the lower slopes of Broadfield Down, however, the south facing slopes are sheltered and sunny and support a range of mixed arable and pastoral agriculture.

The few archaeological overviews to include North Somerset refer to the area's lack of Roman villas, implying that North Somerset, and thus the Yeo valley, is rather a poor cousin to surrounding regions. Nearby Keynsham contains the remains of an opulent villa, its elaborate west wing containing a mosaic-lined corridor and two hexagonal rooms. (Unfortunately, this villa has been largely destroyed by the building of the A4.) The baths at Bath are internationally valued, and are recognised as a world heritage site. Further afield are a range of wealthy, high-status villa sites, such as the palatial, 64-roomed Woodchester villa with its famous Orpheus mosaic in the Cotswolds, and Chedworth, near Cheltenham, one of the largest Roman villas in the UK, well preserved with baths and mosaics.

This chapter, and the fieldwork conducted in the course of it, will attempt to characterise the nature of Romano-British (RB) settlement and land use in the vicinity of Blagdon, and in the surrounding Yeo valley. To enable a clear understanding of the extent of Roman settlement in the area, the following resources have been consulted: North Somerset's Sites and Monuments Record (SMR) listing, antiquarian journals and excavation reports. Additionally, map regression, aerial photographic analysis, and fieldwork such as site visits, field walking and geophysical survey have been conducted. The Yeo valley has never been examined in its entirety, and in fact very little archaeology has been conducted in the valley at all, aside from one significant exception: the 1960s excavations carried out by Peter Fowler of Bristol University at Row of Ashes, Butcombe, and his fieldwork and plotting of associated RB field systems. Fowler's seminal study has meant that Row of Ashes is now a 'type site' for a native British RB farmstead.

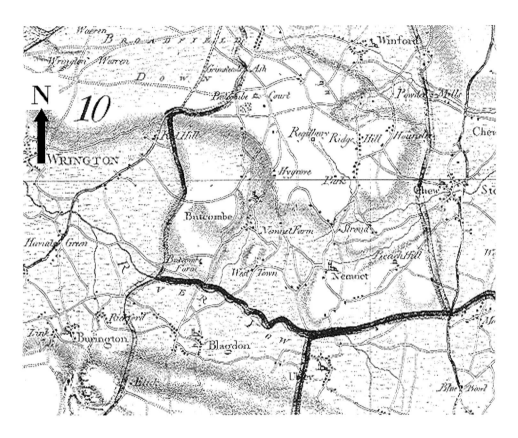

Figure 1: An extract from Day and Master's map of Bristol and Bath, 1782, depicting the Yeo Valley at the end of the eighteenth century.
This map is not drawn to scale, but is nonetheless useful, as it is one of the earliest images of the Yeo Valley.

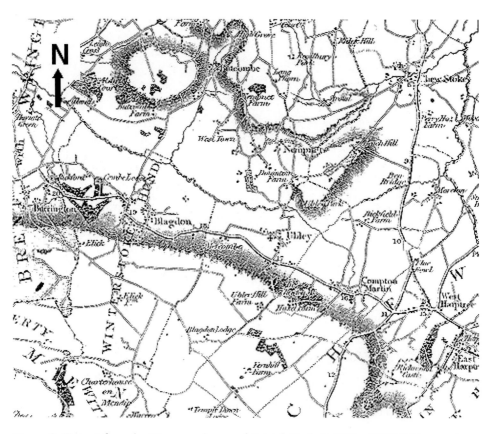

Figure 2: Extract from the Greenwood map of Bristol, Bath & Wells, 1822. This map is not to scale, but does give the sense of Blagdon, and neighbouring villages, as being tucked into the foot slopes of the Mendip hills. The River Yeo is clearly depicted, heading westward from its source at Compton Martin (the map precedes the construction of the Yeo reservoir, which took place in the late nineteenth century).

2.   <u>Romano-British sites in the Yeo valley</u>

This section will detail sites where RB remains are known to be located in the Yeo valley, or where RB material has been recovered. Once all the sites have been described and located, they will be discussed in Section 6, in which possible patterns of settlement and trends of land use will be identified within the study area. In 1993, the owner of Court Farm, **Wrington,** was in the process of constructing a fishpond within the Court garden. During the construction work, the remains of a Romano-British wall came to light immediately west of All Saints' churchyard. The presence of box flue tiles in the wall indicates that it may be the remains of a high-status RB building (Russett, excavation notes, 1993, ASMR 9216.) The wall resembled the exterior of a structure which appeared to continue eastward, into the churchyard. The Romano-British building may be related to the choice of position of the later

Figure 3: Roman patera found near Wrington, 2005.
Photograph courtesy of North Somerset Museum Service.

parish church. Of additional relevance is a wall located in the basement of All Saints' church which is slightly out of alignment with the others. It is possible that this wall may be related to the finds discovered in 1993, although further fieldwork would be needed to determine this. Other evidence of settlement is indicated on North Somerset's SMR: Roman artefacts have been recovered over the years during field-walking near Wrington, including brooches, coins, tiles and Samian ware. In 2005, a first century Roman 'patera', or saucepan, was discovered near Wrington (figure 3). The saucepan was probably used for heating liquids and was part of the standard kit carried by legionary solders. It can be found in domestic and religious contexts. A possible Celtic influence is indicated by the pattern of concentric rings on the bottom of the pan (Portable Antiquities Scheme Annual Report, 2004-05.)

Lye Hole Villa (SMR 668) was originally discovered by tenant William Body in the hot, dry summer of 1876, during which crop marks were clearly visible (PUBSS, 1960, p.33.) Traces of a villa covering half an acre were found and briefly examined in 1876. Material recovered included potsherds, bones, tiles, several tesserae from a pavement, wall plaster, and a hypocaust (under-floor heating system) in which the pilae were made in part with hexagonal roof tiles. Charred wood and evidence of burning revealed that the villa had been destroyed by fire (Page, 1906, p. 308.) The villa had associated rectangular fields which suggest a planned layout of the field system attached to the villa (PUBSS 9, I, 1960, pp.33-5.) Branigan writes, "At Lye Hole the villa appears to have stood within a roughly oblong enclosure of about half an acre which may have protected vegetable plots and fruit trees. ... part of the field system around the villa survives, and is comprised of long, rather narrow, fields only some 30m broad. Eight, or more probably sixteen, fields survive in part, and there were most likely others to the north of those so far recorded if not in other directions too. Even the surviving fragments of the field system suggest a probable annual surplus of seed and consumption requirements of the order of 500 bushels of corn (Branigan, 1976, p. 76.) The evidence therefore reveals that Lye Hole villa was a working farm producing a high yield, possibly even a surplus, presumably to sell. The discoveries in 1876 suggest a site of quite high status, as the villa appeared to have central heating, as indicated by the hypocaust, a mosaic pavement and wall plaster.

Located on the hill slope above Lye Hole Villa (SMR 668) are two native farmsteads: **Scars Farm,** (SMR 671) and **Row of Ashes (**SMR 673). Both were explored by Peter Fowler in the 1960s excavations. Fowler has identified Row of Ashes as a small rural settlement of non-villa type, a 'native farmstead', which has revealed the gradual adoption of Roman practices and building styles by the native British people, with a late Iron Age round house being subsequently replaced by a rectangular structure, and (as one of the first examples of a Romanised native farmstead) Row of Ashes has become a type site (1970, p. 175.) One important aspect of this site revealed by Fowler's excavations is that animal bones discovered on site were mainly from poorer cuts of meat: skull and feet bones comprised the majority of the animal bones discovered, with ox being the largest source of food, followed by sheep and a lesser amount of pig (Fowler, 1969, p.191.) Guy De la Bedoyere has discovered through excavated bone evidence from a wide selection of Roman sites that, in Roman Britain, beef was typically associated with higher status sites, while mutton has been discovered in lower-status contexts (De la Bedoyere, TT, 2006.) The findings at Row of Ashes therefore suggests, not only that livestock farming and butchering were carried out on site, but additionally that the better cuts of meat were presumably raised at Row of Ashes for use by higher-status consumers elsewhere. The nearest large centre of population during RB times was several miles south-east of the farm, at the Roman mining settlement at Charterhouse-on-Mendip. Scars Farm, adjacent to Row of Ashes, is also a native farmstead, and also part of this heavily agricultural landscape of the slopes of Broadfield Down. The aerial photograph in Figure 4, taken before modern agricultural practices had ploughed out the many earthworks, reveals the extent of the farming landscape in this part of the valley. It is fair to suggest that the field systems visible on this photograph may have originally stretched even further.

There is evidence of a villa in **Lower Langford**. Page writes that *The Gentleman's magazine* stated that tiles and part of a blue and red border of a mosaic were uncovered in 1856 at Lower Langford, in digging up the foundations of an old wall. Neale states that, in 1966, Roman remains were discovered in foundation trenches in the grounds of the Veterinary College, at the western end of Lower Langford, by a Mr J.E. Hancock. Neale reports that this site would seem the most likely candidate for the 1856 remains (1970, p.195.) The 'villa' was presumably of some prestige and status, as it contained a mosaic, but unfortunately detailed description and information regarding the site is not available.

A Roman villa near **Havyatt's Green** (SMR 415, grid ref ST 481 614) is listed on the SMR as being discovered when a turnpike road was being built in 1817. The Rev. Preb. H.M. Scarth (1877, p.159) describes the find as having been made by labourers during road alterations. His description also includes details of "limestone walls found eighteen inches down and standing one foot high, roofing tiles and signs of destruction by fire".

Neale has succeeded in re-locating this site after many years of confusion. Her careful research into the alteration of the roadway and her examination of the original letters of Scarth to Skinner has allowed a grid reference to be determined as ST 4801 6145. Neale also has located surface pottery which is dated to the third-fourth centuries, comprising fabrics also found in sealed and dated deposits at Butcombe a few miles to the east (170, p. 199.)

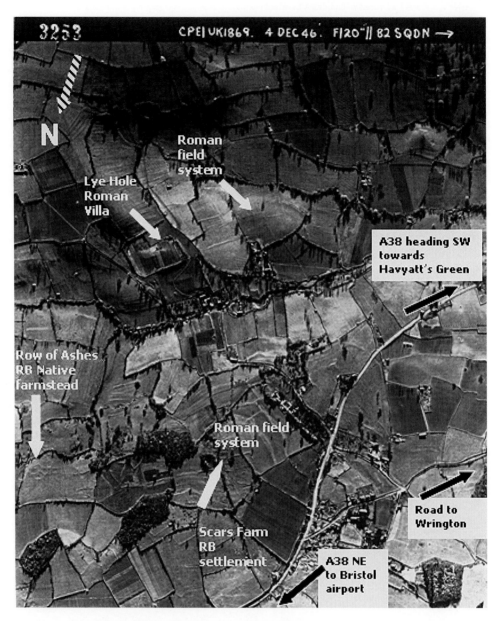

Figure 4: Scars Farm (SMR 668), Row of Ashes (SMR 673) and Lye Hole (SMR 667) are illustrated above. Photograph is oriented with SSE, ie Mendip, at the top. The Romano-British field systems of these three neighbouring sites can be seen over much of the photo. The A38 can be seen running SW down Redhill towards Havyatt's Green. Dec, 1946. English Heritage (NMR) RAF Photography.

Neale's careful analysis succeeded in pinpointing the site of the original road, and the cutting in which a Roman building was discovered, but recent findings suggest that Neale underestimates the full extent of the site: in the course of research for this paper aerial photographic analysis has revealed the crop mark of a large ditched enclosure, measuring about 86m by 103m. The enclosure is rectangular with rounded corners, and is located on a slight rise of land overlooking the Yeo crossing-point of Perry Bridge. The grass within the crop mark is a darker green than the surrounding vegetation, suggesting that the feature is a rectilinear ditch, retaining moisture, thus causing the differential rate of growth (Aston, 2002, p.17.) This ditch may be enclosing a farm site, although this crop mark very much resembles the shape of an early Roman military camp or fort, and its location − on a slight rise by a river crossing − is typical of early forts and reinforces this interpretation of the feature (Welfare & Swan, 1995, p.8-9.) Site visits have recovered a range of RB pottery, including Samian ware, Oxfordshire ware, black-burnished, and local coarse-ware. A rough dating of the shards indicates RB settlement at this site from the first to the fourth century AD. Numismatic finds have also been recovered and range from the first century, with the latest being a clipped coin of Postumus, dating to 269 AD.

Aldwick, a hamlet attached to the village of Butcombe, was recorded as 'Aldwick' in the Domesday Book, and place-name research reveals that 'vic' or 'vicus' is highly likely to refer to a Roman settlement (M. Costen, personal communication, 2004.) Cameron lists 'Aldwick' as meaning 'old farm, with a connection to a Roman site' (1988, pp.147-8.) Field-walking Aldwick, in the field opposite Butcombe Farm (Domesday's 'Aldwick' manor), has recovered a range of material which appears to be of RB date: probable Roman bricks, tiles, and waste from industrial processing of metal, as well as a bronze miscast. This miscast is unlikely to have been brought to Aldwick, and suggests, as does the slag, that some form of industrial processing of metal took place. Most villa sites do contain evidence of some form of light industrial processing occurring onsite. Rather than an even spread across the field, these finds were clustered in specific spreads, and these spreads also included rock and stone building rubble. The quantity of pottery is not as great as could be expected at a 'classic' villa site: it is possible that the finds suggest the presence of ancillary buildings to a villa, with the foundations of the villa itself possibly lying under the current buildings of Butcombe Farm. Alternatively, the settlement may have been an industrial one, processing lead ore mined at the Roman town at Charterhouse-on-Mendip. A further pottery scatter is located only several hundred metres away on North Somerset's SMR, at ST 516 600. Associated with this site is a possible RB field system located just north-east; aerial photographs depict a series of long banks running down the fields, supplying further evidence for Aldwick being the location of a RB settlement. (Figure 5)

Figure 5: Extract from an RAF aerial photograph illustrates the northwest corner of Blagdon Lake. The possible line of Roman road runs west-east near top centre of photo. English Heritage (MNR) RAF Photography.

An associated feature is that of the remains of a disused road, running west-east along the valley side 50 metres above Butcombe Farm. This route-way is visible on aerial photographs from the 1940s, as in figure 5. The route-way skirts the edge of the Sutton plateau, and may have linked Lye Hole or Scars Farm with Roman settlement at Butcombe, implied by the presence of extensive Romano-British field systems. In form and structure the route appears to be of Roman construction: erosion has exposed what appear to be stony foundations, and the land is composed of straight sections, joined by slight kinks, rather than the meandering route taken by most of the local lanes (Figure 5).

Blagdon

Another possible RB settlement site in the Yeo valley is mentioned in Rev. John Skinner's manuscript of 1821, in which he refers to a Roman site in Blagdon. Skinner writes: "On entering Parkfield, we picked up fragments of grey, red and black pottery, also fragments of the pennant roofing stone. I have before noticed that small Roman coins can be found, when digging deep" (BM Add MS 33673, 1821, pp.145-6.) Neale suggests that RB material recorded around 1947 came from grid ref ST 505 590 (CBA Arch Review, 1969, p.45.) Although there are no extant fields going by Skinner's name of 'Park Fields', the 1842 Blagdon tithe map does list a group of four fields with the names of Park Mead, West Park, Lower and Upper East Park, which are likely to be Skinner's Park Fields, as he visited Blagdon only twenty years before the tithe map was drawn up. He describes Park Fields as lying below the church, and he passes them on his way to visit Fairy Toot, in Butcombe.

Figure 6: RAF 1963 Picture NMR Archive. Arrows point to crop-marks of the rectangular feature running NE to SW. Dotted arrows are pointed to NE and SE corners. Notice also the circular feature, signalled by the white arrow. Upper East Park field, Blagdon. 26 July 1963. © **Crown Copyright/MOD.**

Subsequent analysis of aerial photographs taken by the RAF has revealed crop-marks suggesting the presence of remains of a rectangular structure, or series of structures (Figure 6). There have been no known buildings or structures located in Upper East Park: none are depicted on any available map or plan of the area. Consequently, to further investigate the crop marks, a geophysical survey was conducted in October and November 2004. As the survey was seeking to locate sub-soil masonry foundations, a resistivity survey was carried out. Geophysical resistivity surveys measure the amount of moisture in the soil: an electrical current is passed through the ground and the resistance between two probes is measured: the variations in the readings reflect very small differences in the moisture content of the soil. These differences are a result of features under the ground, including archaeological deposits and naturally occurring geology. The survey covered eight grids, each 20m square.

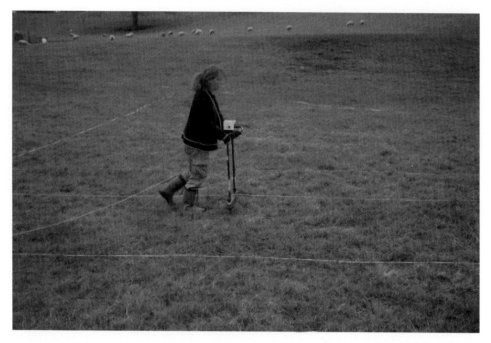

Figure 7. Geophysical survey using twin-probe Resistivity kit. Upper East Park Field, Blagdon,
heading East. Photo: M Follett, Nov. 2004

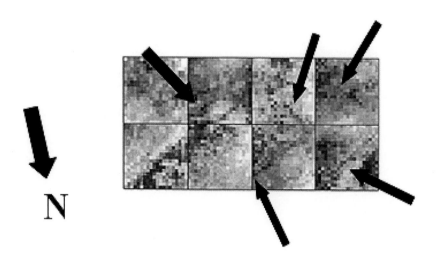

Figure 8: Geophysical survey data from resistivity survey carried out in October and November, 2004.
The dark colour implies buried features of high resistance such as masonry, or rubble, and do not appear
to be related to underlying geology, as the features are regular, and include right-angles. Arrows point to
a possible semi-circular feature; the larger walled enclosure, and what appear to be walls within the larger
enclosure.

The geophysical survey data (figure 8) reveals clearly defined rectilinear areas of high resistance, which suggest the existence of buried remains of a man-made structure. This data revealed a similar sized structure to that suggested by the aerial photographic analysis of crop marks visible in RAF photographs. Tentative interpretation suggests a series of rectilinear enclosures measuring approximately 20m in width, with an overall enclosure of roughly 40m in width. These features may possibly consist of stone, rubble or other hardcore material, as the reading indicates high resistance. Within these enclosures, there appears to possibly be smaller rectilinear structures, one with what appears to be a semi-circular shape, forming what could possibly be described as an apsidal end, measuring approximately 12m in width, which again appears to be constructed of masonry or other material providing high resistance. Some of the areas of high resistance are well defined linear features, of about one metre in width, which may indicate wall remains; while other, broader, areas of high resistance could be interpreted as building collapse, that is the spread of wall or roofing rubble. These structures appear to measure between five and ten metres in width. Height is impossible to determine without further investigation of the site, although it is fair to say that the dimensions, arrangement and shape of these features resemble that of a large, stone-constructed occupation site, with a large enclosure containing several buildings. While it is impossible to assess the findings with any degree of certainty, it is possible that the feature revealed by the survey data might be the remains of a Romano-British site, perhaps that which Skinner noted. Further investigation is required to further the survey data by targeted keyhole excavation in an effort to retrieve datable material.

The feature at Upper East Park is located in a north facing position, and if it *is* found to be a RB site, local parallels can be found for north-facing sites in the Yeo valley. South facing positions would normally be more sought after as they receive more sunlight and are therefore warmer and lighter. North Somerset's SMR reveals that Romano-British building material indicating a possible Romano-British building has been found at the site of Springhead Farm, Upper Langford, and Roman artefacts ranging from a glass bottle and a bracelet to tuyere (from a furnace) have been found in the garden of the farm. It may be that the Roman occupation site is now covered by the later farmhouse. Given the north-facing aspect of Springhead Farm, it is perhaps surprising that a Roman building was constructed here. On the other hand, assets of the site, including a powerful and plentiful spring, and large swathes of ancient woodland, may have made up for any disadvantages to the north-facing aspect of the site. Adjacent to the farm is an associated Romano-British field system, stretching northwards to the Mendip forest, suggesting that the potential villa site may have been surrounded by a contemporary field system. The RB site at Springhead Farm, Upper Langford, is in much the same aspect as our suspected site at Upper East Park. The close proximity of Upper East Park to the known RB settlement at Charterhouse, the sheltered location, the well appointed site on fertile farmland, and close proximity to a spring, do nothing to detract from the possibility that this site has a RB origin. Were excavation to establish that this is an RB site, an important point would need to be addressed: where are the route ways from this site to other RB sites in the vicinity? If this suggested site is verified, it would dovetail with archaeologist Peter Fowler's theory that each Saxon parish in the Yeo valley contained a Roman estate. Blagdon had been a 'hole' in Fowler's theory, as such a site in Blagdon parish has been 'missing'.

Of additional relevance may be the presence of the extant spring 'Lower Well', an abundant and reliable clean water source, located immediately above Upper East Park. The spring is situated on a tiny apportionment of common land and has an odd concave stone wall behind it, which has become embedded in the retaining wall, located on the upward slope of Park Farm's boundary. This concave wall is very much like a smaller version of the still-extant wall behind the water shrine created at the natural spring at Chedworth Roman villa (Pers.obs, 2004.) It is possible, indeed probable, that *if* the remains in Upper East Park are of an occupation site then the spring at Lower Well would have been used by the occupants, as the spring is located directly above our site. The spring at Chedworth was used by the villa occupants as the sole water source, as well as being a shrine. Quinn states that Blagdon villagers traditionally shunned Lower Well, in the belief that it was contaminated by the nearby churchyard, and another local well, Timsell (west of the church), was used instead (1999, p.163.) Given that the churchyard is equidistant from both Timsell and Lower Well, there may be another explanation for this reluctance; it is conceivable that this belief is a corruption of earlier knowledge that Lower Well was once a RB water shrine, and it may be that these pagan connections lead early Christian villagers to associate the well with unclean water.

Before we discuss how these sites fit into a pattern in the Yeo valley, we need to first turn to the mining settlement at Charterhouse, in order to establish a possible relationship between the two locations.

3.   Roman mining settlement at Charterhouse-on-Mendip

The Roman mining settlement at Charterhouse was producing lead ingots ('pigs') by AD 49, just six years after the invasion in AD 43. Lead ingots and coins date the settlement from the early years of the invasion to the late fourth century. Lead mining took place here in Roman times, and lead was used for many purposes. It was easily worked as it has a low melting point, and was used for water-pipes, cisterns, coffins and burial urns, among many other purposes (Scullard, 1979, p.133.) The toxic properties of lead were not recognised in Roman times, and it is recorded that lead acetate (known as the 'sugar of lead') was deliberately added to sweeten wine. Despite Knight's comments that "it is hardly likely that anything but the search for lead and silver could have reconciled them to life in a spot so barren and remote and desolate" (1977, p.519), Charterhouse was more than a rough mining outpost: artefacts recovered at the site include elaborate locks, keys, small masks, bells, spoons, tweezers and hairpins, and engraved gems with carvings of Mars, Minerva, Mercury, and 'Cupid soldiers' (these may have been set in iron signet rings). In 1872, two very finely cut carnelians (a type of quartz, with deep red translucent colour) were found in Townfield, Charterhouse. One is of a helmeted warrior, maybe Mars, with shield and spear; the other has the two graceful figures of a 'youth and maid', and is described as possibly being from an engagement ring (Knight, pp.511-15.) Samian ware (high status ceramic imported from Gaul) has been found at Charterhouse, as well as hypocaust tiles (used in the central heating of Roman houses), which have been discovered within a field wall in Lower Rains Batch, implying that there were houses of some note within the settlement (CHERT, 2004.)

Evidence exists for the dating of the settlement at Charterhouse from the prehistoric, and stretches right up to the end of the fourth century. Todd's 1993 excavation at an earthwork enclosure at Charterhouse has revealed what he believes to be evidence for Iron Age lead working on Mendip (1993, p.63.) Pre-Roman lead mining and trading of this ore may account for the rapidity with which the Roman administration was able to identify the rich vein of mineral ore on Mendip. Dates inscribed on ingots can assist in depicting the speed at which the Roman mining got under way: one ploughed up in 1853 can be dated by its inscription to AD 49 (Knight, p.516.) The dates on the ingots and coins, and the shape of the fort, combine to make Charterhouse one of the earliest established settlements following the Roman invasion of 43 AD. Although the name of the Romano-British settlement at Charterhouse is not known, part of the name has been tentatively identified from one of the ingots containing the letters 'Veb', which possibly refers to the settlement's prehistoric roots (Palmer, 1961.) The latest inscribed ingots from the Mendips belong to AD 164-9, and, although only 115 years are covered by the dates on the ingots, evidence from finds of coins reveal that occupation continued until the mid fourth century, with even a few late fourth century silver coins being found (Scullard, p.131.)

The size of the population of the Roman town at Charterhouse, and therefore its attendant needs in terms of foodstuffs, has never been calculated. Faulkner's re-assessment of the physical limits of the settlement demonstrates that the street grid extends beyond the limits recognised by the scheduling and convincingly locates a possible Roman-British temple (Faulkner, unpublished MA dissertation, 1997, p.28.) Additionally, a geophysical survey carried out in July 2005 by GSB Prospection as part of Channel 4's 'Big Roman Dig' has revealed the continued presence of streets and building platforms across Town Field and continuing southwest into the field of Cowleaze. However, Faulkner's re-assessment, and the recent geophysical survey, although very useful, do not go far enough in revealing the accurate character and dimensions of the Roman town. Further fieldwork has located an area of regular high resistance south-east of the Roman amphitheatre, the dimensions of which resemble large public stone buildings. Additionally, aerial photographic analysis has identified a crop mark resembling a theatre, on the slopes of Lower Rains Batch (Watson, 2002.) These discoveries, in conjunction with Faulkner's work, suggest that Charterhouse may have been a town of some note with a diverse and cultured population, and may not deserve its reputation as a 'wild west' town, rough, industrial, and lacking indicators of higher status.

What then is the relationship which grew up between the Roman town at Charterhouse and the Yeo valley? Did settlements in the valley benefit from having this resource of lead in the area, and did the settlement in the upland zone similarly benefit from the sheltered agricultural resources of the valley? Whatever the relationship was, the link needs to be established, to identify the physical means for the two distinct areas to exchange goods. Given the lead content of the soil, and the widespread mining activity at Charterhouse, it is yet unclear how the residents were supplied with food, as it seems unlikely that they would be able to produce their own. Crops may not have grown well on top of Mendip due to the poisonous effect of the lead and associated processing. (In fact, toxicity from the lead mining is still present today: an archaeological excavation carried out in July 2005, as part of Time Team's Big Roman Dig was abruptly curtailed when extremely high readings of cadmium, lead and arsenic were discovered in the soil.) It was not a suitable environment for agriculture and crops, and is likely to have been detrimental to the health of grazing animals, such as horses. The mining settlement would therefore have needed supplies from the farming estates in the valleys, and route-ways by which to transport it. Where then, are these route-ways?

Figure 9: Charterhouse Roman settlement: The irregular grid of holloways, which are the remains of the Roman streets of the settlement, are visible along the right hand edge of the photograph. There are two possible routes which appear to extend beyond the grid north towards Blagdon, Route A and Route B. The solid white line is a public footpath, and the proposed routes are picked out in dotted white line. It appears that the westerly route, route A, follows the line of the public footpath and then Two Trees road towards the west end of the village; while the easterly route, Route B, appears to follow a holloway north of the Roman settlement, crosses the B3134, and joins with the line of the public footpath which comes up the Score past Leaze Farm. (The earthwork visible at the bottom centre of the photograph is recorded on Somerset's SMR as possibly being a small earthen Roman amphitheatre, although this has not been proven conclusively.) Centred on ST 502 567. Vertical composite, OGS Crawford, 1931. English Heritage (NMR) Crawford Collection.

4.   Communication and transportation in the Yeo valley

The settlement at Charterhouse, as depicted on the Ordnance Survey (OS) historical map of Roman Britain, is located at the end of the Roman road from 'Old Sarum' (near Salisbury), which crossed the Fosse Way north of Shepton Mallet. This depiction assumes that goods were delivered along this westward spur off the Fosse Way, and that lead went out along the same road, but the Roman settlement at Charterhouse, as already suggested, had a need for supplies and products from suppliers in the valley, and, in turn, the valley appears to have had a range of farming based settlements which seem to have developed and increased during the Roman period. Therefore the two geographical zones appear to be interconnected. There is a well-documented route from Charterhouse to the north east: Williams describes the well-attested Roman road, Stratford Lane, which travels from Charterhouse, down the Mendip slope to Chew Park Villa, coinciding with the old parish boundary between Ubley and West Harptree, and possibly extending onward towards Gold Cross, where a further Roman site is known (1992, p.151-82.) A further route-way has been identified by John Knight of Bristol University, and is in close proximity to the field system previously referred to south of Nempnett church (cited by Dunn, 2004.) This roadway is evident in aerial photography, and runs north–north-east/south–south-west to the east of Nempnett church. A segment of this route is aligned with the parish boundary. This suggested road is formed of straight sections connected by slight kinks. Knight inspected the construction and line of this road, which appears to head directly north–north-east for the Roman port of Abonae (Sea Mills), and the road appears to have been solidly and well constructed. Study of aerial photographs and historic maps suggests that the Nempnett Roman road continued to the south-south-west, and veered west at the steep Mendip slope at Ubley, cut up Ubley Drove, and thus continued to the mining establishment. If this is the case, this line is also the course of the original parish boundary of Ubley and Blagdon. Given the solid construction and line of the road, it is fair to speculate that this road most likely *would* have continued along this proposed route, as it is rather unlikely to have abruptly ended at the footsteps of Broadfield Down. This road may have been used both to bring supplies up to the town, and to take lead ingots to the port at Abonae. Bird suggests Abonae linked the area to other destinations in the UK and on the continent (1986, p.53-4.) This would appear a much more direct route for export, than via land to south coast ports, especially given the weight of the ingots.

A further road can be suggested: if the site at Upper East Park, Blagdon is indeed a RB site, either villa or native farmstead, it would have most likely been linked with some sort of route-way to enable goods to be transported to the mining settlement. Rev. John Skinner made various observations about Blagdon in his diary, early in the nineteenth century, describing a 'Roman road' running from the Roman settlement at Charterhouse, down to Blagdon, and along towards Butcombe, continuing towards

Bristol. Skinner mentions the name of the road as 'Portway' several times in his discussion of this road.

Cameron's *English Place Names* states that 'one particular stretch of Roman road, the continuation of the London-Silchester Road, is called Port Way. This is a common name, more often used of old track-ways – some of prehistoric date. In most cases, however, the name is no longer used of the track itself and survives only in the names of farms. The meaning is 'way leading to a town', though it is rarely possible today to be certain which town is meant (Cameron, 1961, p.157.)

There are no longer any roads within the vicinity of Blagdon or Butcombe referred to by the name of 'Portway', and at first glance it appears that there is only one road down from Charterhouse, the road of 'Two Trees', which heads north-west down off the Mendip plateau to the western edge of Blagdon village. This would by no means be a direct route between Upper East Park and the mining town at Charterhouse, but does appear to form part of 'Route A' as illustrated above. However, Crawford's 1931 aerial photograph (figure 9) does suggest that the network of roads at Charterhouse may descend the hill to the north, as does Day and Master's 1782 map (figure 1.)

It is apparent from the orientation of the cottages and farms along Church Street, that the current main road through Blagdon is not the original route through the village, as the older cottages and farms at East End are 'side-on' to the Bath road, and face the lanes running north-south through the village: Church Street and Street End. Blagdon is a polyfocal village, that is it has more than one centre. The various neighbourhoods are referred to as 'East End', 'West End' and 'Street End', all of which are on a north-south axis. Leaving the Roman settlement at Charterhouse, the holloway leading out of the Roman town can be seen on figure 9. If this is followed northward, it leads to the side of an anomalous triangular shaped field, adjacent to Upper Rains Batch. Following this, a holloway can be seen running through two fields, and meeting the start of a public footpath (personal observation, 2005.) This right of way continues down the Mendip slope until it reaches a series of holloways leading to the Score. The Score is the old south-north access for Blagdon, and crosses the A368 road to join Church Street. This, then, is tentatively the vital link between Charterhouse and Blagdon, but even so it at first appears that the route to the 'villa' site is still not direct, as Church Street meanders northwards down Park Batch, and would be a very indirect route to the site at Upper East Park. However, careful examination of now lost field boundaries suggests the remains of a roadway fossilised in the field boundaries existing in 1842, as illustrated on Blagdon's tithe map, creating a very direct route to Upper East Park. Evidence contained in the apportionment records reveals that houses now on Grib Lane were listed as being on Easton Town Street, suggesting that what is currently referred to as Church Street, or East End Lane, as it was known in the eighteenth century, was positioned to the east of its

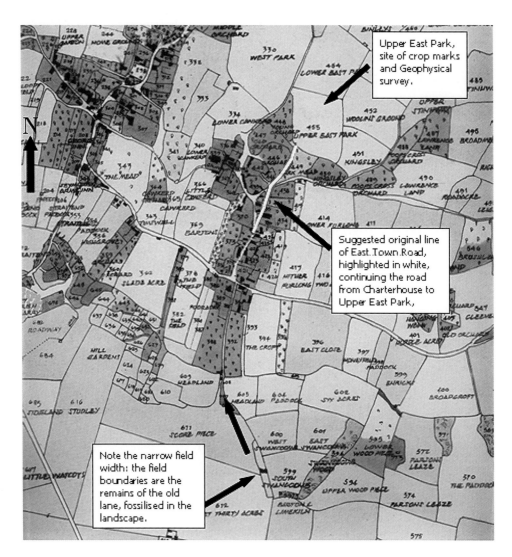

Figure 10: Blagdon Tithe Map, 1842, showing the continuation of the route-way, down the Score, over the A368; along between cottages lots, and down to Upper East Park. Tithe Map courtesy of Rob Marley, BLHS.

current location (Blagdon Apportionment, 1842.) Blagdon's tithe map reveals a very short section of lane in front of apportionment 438; this lane crosses Grib Lane and runs north-east, again very briefly (Figure 10.)

However, the field boundary as revealed on Blagdon tithe map, between the field called 'Orchard' and 'Park Mead', continues the line of this lane and curves down the hill, ending at an odd shaped portion of Park Mead which juts to the north-west. The small segment of the field may be the neck of the, now long invisible, lane. The brief lane in front of lot 438, as illustrated on the tithe map, is now the site of a very long front garden with raised beds. It is rare for the older cottages in Blagdon to have front gardens, as most front onto the lanes. A site visit revealed a very interesting combination of factors: a short section of lane was found running to the west of 'Old Cottages', lot 435. The line of this road appears to have previously headed into the front garden of 'Wisteria Cottage'. Progress along this lane, however, is blocked by a short section of wall, beyond which is the front garden of Wisteria Cottage, and at this point the lane veers abruptly to the left. It is suggested that the course of Church Street, at some point in the past (certainly predating the tithe map of 1842), had a more easterly course than it has now, a course which took it directly from the heart of the Roman settlement at Charterhouse, down the north slopes of Mendip, down the Score, down 'East Town Street', running immediately in front of Wisteria Cottage, to the left of Old Cottages, to the right of Lamorna Cottage, across the current line of Grib Lane, then curving down the slope, following the current property line of Lake House, to the gated entrance of Upper East Park, and to the feature discovered by resistivity survey and aerial analysis, as previously described.

This evidence suggests a direct route from the suspected villa site to the Roman mining town at Charterhouse-on-Mendip (Figure 11). This may in fact explain why old documents do not refer to the lane as Church Lane: the church was in the middle of the village, with the settlement of West Town and East Town either side of it. Deeds belonging to Lamorna Cottage reveal that the adjacent cottage dates to 1656. Therefore the lane must have been realigned prior to this date, thus allowing the house to be built upon the old roadway. While this evidence implies that a route-way existed in the past, directly from the Roman town at Charterhouse down to the suspected villa site in Upper East Park, it does not prove that the lane was in use during the RB period, but it certainly is a strong possibility. This suggestion is supported by the discovery in 1858 of a lead ingot on the northern slopes of Mendips in Blagdon. The ingot appears to have been lost while in transit, or was perhaps deliberately hidden with the intention of being returned for at a later date (SANHS, 1858, pp.16-18.) Additionally, a Roman coin was discovered in the area now referred to as East Croft, Blagdon, in the 1940s (this is along the line of the proposed 'Route B'), and a second Roman coin was discovered near St Andrew's Church in the early 1990s.

Figure 11: North-south route through Blagdon: The Score heading south up Mendip towards Charterhouse, December 1946; English Heritage (NMR) RAF photography.

5.   Romano-British settlement patterns in the Yeo valley

Pre-Roman occupation

The first association to emerge in seeking patterns for RB settlement in the Yeo valley is that Iron Age tribes were clearly living and farming in the area before the Roman occupation of AD 43. Excavation evidence from Row of Ashes, Lye Hole Villa, and the neighbouring villa in the Chew valley (Chew Park villa) all demonstrate the presence of Iron Age (IA) activity. As archaeological excavation has been limited in the Yeo valley we are unable to determine whether this pattern is true for all our sites. However, the trend can certainly be identified as occurring wherever excavation has been carried out. The proposed Upper East Park site may fit this pattern as well, as aerial photography reveals a circular crop mark, which may be a possible IA hut circle, adjacent to the stone built features. This evidence is obviously very speculative, but is worth considering, and should archaeological investigation be pursued at Upper East Park it is one question for which an answer should be attempted.

Types of RB settlement

During Romano-British times, the economy was predominantly an agricultural one, and one of the most profound effects of the Roman occupation was the development of the landscape for more intensive agricultural purposes. Evidence exists for the increase in agriculture at the time of the Roman invasion. Hill and Ireland state that, "Given the need to feed the army of occupation, which at first must have had to import significant quantities of foodstuffs, as well as the newly established economy of Britain immediately after the conquest, the great change during the Roman occupation was in terms of the extent and type of land which could be turned to arable use." Hill and Ireland cite the better availability of iron tools, and increased use of drainage, as fundamental in the intensification of agriculture during the Roman period. The effect of these changes caused "significant alteration to the long-static British landscape and a shift from short term subsistence to stable surplus in agricultural terms" (1996, p.83.) Hill and Ireland attribute the many changes to the British countryside, including the introduction of a range of root crops (including turnip, carrots and parsnips, and new varieties of bean, peas, celery, and cabbage) to the need to help sustain herds throughout the winter, and therefore to preclude the need for culling (1996, p.84.) Thus the flocks would not be depleted by spring, thereby allowing the development of surpluses of dairy products and wool.

Although the term 'villa' suggests the opulence inherent in painted wall plaster, hot baths, under-floor heating, and mosaic tiled floors, at its essence the term simply refers to a farm or farming estate or establishment, some with an area surrounded by a ditched or walled enclosure, and possibly with outbuildings for animals. Johnston states that villas were seldom a single building, however luxurious that building may be (1994, p.18.) A water source would have been essential, which may have been a spring or well. Therefore, villas were essentially 'Romanised' IA farmsteads. Current evidence suggests that the Yeo valley contains a number of Romano-British farmsteads with associated field systems, although these field systems do differ in appearance.

Evidence reveals that villas were sometimes built directly on top of, or adjacent to, previous Iron Age structures, suggesting continuity of site use, as the native population eventually adopted the new style of building. A type-site example of this is the site at Row of Ashes in Butcombe: rectilinear buildings were built adjacent to earlier round houses. Row of Ashes demonstrates continuity of land use, and the adoption of new designs of domestic buildings at a low economic level of society. It is possible that further Romano-British sites lie unidentified in the Yeo valley: using Ireland and Hill's definitions of field systems, the field system in Nempnett, as discussed above, resembles that associated with a villa, and it may be that the field name evidence, and location of the Nempnett Roman road, indicate the possible presence of a villa site located in the region south of Nempnett church, on the south-facing slopes of Broadfield Down, as suggested by Dunn. Given the presence of the five springs at that location, this could be a realistic suggestion, and, if Fowler's suggested pattern of one Roman estate per ancient Saxon parish boundary is correct, then it is likely that such a site is in existence.

Romanisation

Settlement in the Yeo valley did adopt a Romanised way of life fairly rapidly, in terms of agricultural intensification. Considering the early arrival of the occupying army at Charterhouse, the settlement sites at Havyatt Green and Lye Hole, for which we have datable evidence, reveal that, strikingly, although farming is very likely to have increased during the Roman occupation, development of these sites into recognizable villa sites was very late. Comparisons with the RB sites in the Chew Valley demonstrate that there too, the villa was constructed in the later half of the third century, and Rahtz believes it may have been occupied for only one generation (Rahtz, 1977, p.18.) In fact Branigan concludes that almost all the villas in the canton of the western Belgai (the name given to the local Iron Age tribe of the Dubonni by the Roman administration) for which there is any notable dating evidence, prove to be late third or early fourth century foundation (1976, p.42.) Additionally, looking to the south of Mendip, the pottery found in excavations at Cheddar vicarage, along with villa building debris, dates to the same period (Brannigan, 1976, p.42.) Therefore the villas at Havyatt, Lye Hole, Cheddar and Chew Park are all of a similarly late construction date.

The style of Roman construction most probably reflected the status and wealth of the owner. Small simple corridor 'villas' may not have been any more practical or comfortable than an Iron Age round house, but may have been adopted out of a desire to 'Romanise' and to fit in with this introduced way of life. While some residents may have very quickly chosen to adopt the Roman style of buildings, perhaps as a status or wealth indicator, other native residents may have chosen deliberately *not* to copy the Roman style of building, perhaps out of principle or tradition. Without central heating, a stone-build construction heated solely by portable brazier is likely to have been colder and more uncomfortable than a round house with central fire. While it may have been a political statement not to adopt Romanised building and construction style, it could have been just a practical decision. Central heating required hypocaust tiles, a furnace, a large volume of fuel, and a slave or other worker to continually stoke the fire. For all but wealthy families, this is likely to have been a heavy drain on resources and finances.

Lead

Local metal detectorists have discovered finds on the 'fort' site at Perry Bridge described earlier, such as Roman coins, including a clipped coin of Postumus, dating to 259-269 AD, and a large quantity of lead objects, including splashes of lead, miscasts, pot plugs, lead weight, casts, and strips and coils of lead. The discovery of lead 'roll', in figure 12, suggests flashing for roofing, or plumbing, while the large number of lead splashes reveals extensive on-site use of lead, as the 'splashes' are unlikely to have been brought to the site. It is fair to suggest that this quantity of lead splashes probably reflects light industrial processes, which in turn implies the movement of lead down off the hill and into the valley. In addition, field walking at this site during the course of this study has located a full range of Romano-British ceramic at this site, including Samian ware, grey ware, Oxfordshire ware, a large quantity of pennant roofing tiles, and large building stone, which, although undatable, is possibly the remains of the villa, due to the other material found with it. While it is unfair to state that the lead material recovered at this site definitely dates to RB times, the complete absence of medieval or late medieval pottery, combined with the presence of a range of RB material, does suggest this to be the case.

Figure 12: Clockwise from middle top: Lead weight, lead sheeting; cast; and two pot plugs from field West of Perry Bridge.
(Loan of artefacts courtesy of Nick Baker. Photo: S Watson, Nov. 2004)

Location of Romano-British sites

The presence of RB sites on the north facing slopes of Mendip suggests that land may have been in great demand. As we have discussed above, it is likely that the Roman settlement at Charterhouse may have needed of lot of foodstuffs to support the industry there. Crops, dairy, beef, pigs, and the need for the stabling and care of horses (for which there would have been a large demand at Charterhouse, given the heavy work of lead production and transportation), may have had to be met off the hilltop, in view of the environment of Mendip and the toxic presence of lead in the soil. It is also fair to comment that the locations on the south side of the Yeo valley, although north-facing, may have been convenient for the farmers, as the north-facing slope was nearest to the mining settlements on Mendip.

Peter Fowler postulates a link between local parish boundaries and the boundaries of Romano-British estates, based on the fact that each parish appears to have one villa within it. This study has found evidence to suggest that the settlement pattern described here is consistent with Fowler's theory, with one main villa existing per parish. On occasion, villa estates also had associated smaller farms, or native farmsteads associated with them. The Yeo valley is characterised by smaller farms, with metalworking taking place off the hill. From these known sites, we can surmise that Romano-British occupation of the Yeo valley consists not only of farms providing sustenance to the mining town at Charterhouse, but also higher-status sites in their own right. The complex patterns and phasing of landscape use and occupation during Romano-British times suggest that the valley was heavily farmed and well occupied, perhaps more so than previously acknowledged.

6.   **Conclusions**

The evidence suggests that Blagdon and the rest of the Yeo valley was occupied and farmed in Roman times. Charterhouse, seemingly isolated from other contemporary settlements, was clearly not isolated in the Roman period. This is very useful, as not only does it suggest that farm supplies could have been transported to Mendip, but it also explains the presence of lead artefacts in the lowland areas, and allows the possibility that the lead and silver may have been transported northwards, without having to head east towards the Fosse Way. Evidence from field-walking (Blagdon, Aldwick) and metal detected finds (Perry Bridge) reveal that lead working took place in the valley. Whether this is a reflection of the fact that lead is easy to work with on a small scale, as a furnace is not needed (just a crucible and a fire, as the melting point of lead is relatively low), or whether light industry of another sort was occurring, is unclear at the present, as current evidence is too limited to reveal an answer. The role of lead in the Yeo valley has been highly underrated in regard to the link it provides with Charterhouse. The presence of the suspected fort at Perry Bridge, and lead workings, implies that lead was brought unprocessed off Mendip, to be worked, cast, and either used locally, or possibly shipped out to the Bristol Channel, thus adding a new dimension to the settlement of the Yeo valley. The large settlement at Charterhouse meant there were new markets for agricultural surplus. Despite Rahtz's assertion that the Chew Villa supplied all or most of the food supplies needed for Charterhouse (1977, p.15), the evidence discussed here suggests that much of the Yeo valley was also farmed in order to supply produce to the mining settlement. This intensification of agriculture is likely to have been in response to need. One striking aspect of the Yeo valley is the fact that there was very early Roman settlement (as lead ingots from Charterhouse date to AD 47) but late adoption of Roman values and Romanization. It had a mixed farming population with native farmsteads, and villas appearing late in the third century. Additionally, an early 'fortlet' at Perry Bridge at an important river crossing maintained control early on, while later metal working and possible use of the river for transport occurred.

Settlements along the southern edge of the Yeo valley, although north-facing, were sheltered from the prevailing south-westerly winds. Furthermore, the significance of these new sites, such as the possible early military camp or fort by Perry Bridge, the villa site in Blagdon, and further road networks connecting the hilltop with Blagdon and the northern valley side, support Fowler's hypothesis that the parish boundaries reflect the much older landholdings of RB estates. Fowler's theory means that Blagdon, in order to fit into the pattern, should have a villa within its parish boundaries, and our fieldwork results suggest that the proposed site at Upper East Park is the 'missing' site.

The valley lies at an interesting junction of land use: of the Levels, the heights of Mendip and Broadfield Down, and the fertile valley floor. This rich provision of varied topography and geology does appear to have influenced the subsequent development of RB settlement. It is, however, the Yeo valley's distinctive spring line, edging along both the north and the south sides of the valley, providing clean, reliable and abundant spring water year-round, which influenced settlement patterns, as it is along this line that the RB occupation sites lay. It is therefore reasonable to speculate that it may be that a source of clean drinking water was more important than a south-facing aspect. It is not so much lack of villas and other types of RB settlement, but rather a lack of investigation and excavation which has contributed to the Yeo valley's low profile in terms of its Romano-British past. Distinctive and unique, the Yeo valley deserves more attention and carefully targeted excavation, to reveal more details about the complexity of the valley's past. Blagdon's role in the Roman occupation of Britain, therefore, seems to fit into the pattern of the Yeo valley as a whole. Skinner's discoveries of Roman pottery and coins, the crop marks and geophysical survey, and Crawford's 1931 aerial photograph revealing holloways leading towards Blagdon which link up with existing right of ways, all provide evidence of Blagdon's involvement with this period of Britain's history. What is probable is that, despite changes in the landscape over the past (roughly) 1,700 years, aspects of the village which are currently valued may also have been appreciated in Roman Britain.

So, to return to our initial question: what was happening in and around Blagdon during the Roman occupation? The area which is now Blagdon parish appears to have had a similar size in terms of estate boundary. The village provided sheltered, spring-fed fertile land, suitable for arable and livestock farming, with fresh, clean air, close enough to the Roman mining town at Charterhouse to enable ease of trade, but removed from the smoke and pollution.

Acknowledgements

Thanks to Mary Mead of Yeo Valley Farms; Sir David Wills of the Wills Estate; and ACF Hospitality, Aldwick, for generous access to their land. Thanks also to Nick Baker, Conservation Officer at Alvis Brothers Farms; Vince Russett, North Somerset County Archaeology Officer, for information and access to SMR files; Simon Moth, Conservation Officer at Yeo Valley Farms, for his assistance; Rob Marley for the use of his reproduction of Blagdon's tithe map; Sue Marley for her assistance with apportionment and census records; and Sheila Johnson for access to the aerial photographic archive. Thanks to Mark Corney and Josh Pollard for identification of RB material recovered during field-walking; to Spike Follett and Tom Watson-Follett for assistance with geophysical survey work; and to Charlie Oscroft, Shirley Payne, and Donna Cox for assistance with childcare.

Illustrations

Figure 1: Day and Master's map of Bristol and Bath, 1782. Not drawn to scale

Figure 2: The Greenwood map, of Bristol, Bath & Wells, 1822. Not drawn to scale

Figure 3: Roman Patera, Wrington, North Somerset Museum Service

Figure 4: Lye Hole; Scars Farm and Row of Ashes Roman sites. RAF CPE/UK1869. Frame: 3253. 4 DEC 1946. English Heritage, (NMR) RAF Photography.

Figure 5: Aldwick, North of Blagdon lake. RAF 1946, Ref: CPE/UK 1869, Frame no: 1258 Dated: 4 Dec 1946. English Heritage, (NMR) RAF Photography

Figure 6: Upper East Park, Blagdon. Reference: 543/2332 FR: 0306 IF 21 Date: 26 July 1963. © Crown Copyright/MOD. Reproduced with the permission of the Controller of Her Majesty's Stationery Office

Figure 7: Geophysical survey using resistivity. ST 507 591. Upper East Park, Blagdon

Figure 8: Geophysical survey data from resistivity survey, Upper East Park, Blagdon

Figure 9: Charterhouse Romano-British mining settlement, looking west, with Town Field visible to left mid ground. Centred on ST 503 564, English Heritage (NMR) Crawford Collection, 1931.

Figure 10: Blagdon Tithe Map, 1842, Copyright: Rob Marley, BLHS

Figure 11: The Score, Blagdon, heading south up Mendip towards Charterhouse-on-Mendip. RAF photo, 1946, NMR RAF/CPE/UK/1869; Frame No: 3269; 4 DEC 1946; English Heritage (NMR) RAF photography.

Figure 12: Clockwise from middle top: Lead weight, lead sheeting; cast; and two pot plugs from Field west of Perry Bridge. Photograph: S. Watson

Abbreviations

BLHS: Blagdon Local History Society
BM: British Museum
CBA: Council of British Archaeology
IA: Iron Age
NMR: National Monument Record Centre
NSCC: North Somerset County Council
OS: Ordnance Survey
PUBSS: Proceedings of the University of Bristol Spelaeological Society
RB: Romano-British
SANHS: Somerset Archaeology and Natural History Society
SMR: Sites and Monuments Record

Bibliography

'Archaeological notes: Lye Hole Roman villa', in *Proceedings of the University of Bristol Spelaeological Society*, vol.IX, no.1 (1960), pp.33-5.

Aston, M. *Interpreting the landscape from the air* (Stroud, 2002)
Avon County Council Planning Dept. *Avon's past from the air* (1984)

De la Bedoyere, G. *Roman towns in Britain* (B. T. Batsford Ltd/ English Heritage, 1992).

Bowden (Ed). *Unravelling the landscape* (Stroud, 1999)

British Geological Survey, Wells Sheet 280, Solid and Drift Edition, 1: 50,000.

Branigan, K. *The Roman villa in South-West England* (Bradford-on-Avon, 1976)

Cameron, K. *English place names* (Batsford, 1988)

Cartwright, M.A. 'A sketch of the history of Butcombe', in *Proceedings of the Bath Natural History and Antiquarian Field Club*, vol. III (1877), pp.25-34.

Croft, R. & Aston, M. *Somerset from the air* (Somerset County Council, 1993.)

Davies, Hugh. *Roads in Roman Britain* (Tempus, 2002.)

Dunn, Richard. *Nempnett Thrubwell: barrows, names and manors* (Dorset, 2004.)

Faulkner, D. *Charterhouse: a Roman town reconsidered.* (Unpublished MA thesis, University of Bristol, 1997.)

Fowler, P.J. 'Excavation of a Romano-British settlement at Row of Ashes Farm, Butcombe, North Somerset: interim report 1966-67', in *Proceedings of the University of Bristol Spelaeological Society*, vol. 2 (1965-6), pp.209236.

Fowler, P.J. (ed) Council for British Archaeology archaeological review, no. 1 (1966); no. 2 (1967); no. 3 (1968); no. 4 (1969)

Fowler, P.J. 'Fieldwork and excavation in the Butcombe Area, North Somerset: second interim report, 1968-9', in *Proceedings of the University of Bristol Spelaeological Society,* vol.12, no.2 (1970), pp.169-194.

Goudie, A., & Gardiner, R. *Discovering landscapes in England and Wales* (George Allen & Unwin, 1985).

Hunt T.J., & Dawe P.N. (eds). *Notes & queries for Somerset and Dorset*, vol.XXVII (1961), pp.197-99.

Johnston, David E. *Roman villas* (Shire Archaeology, 1994.)

Jones, B., & Mattingley, D. *An atlas of Roman Britain* (Child Publishing, 1990)

Knight, F.A. *The heart of Mendip* (1915.)

Leach, Peter. *Roman Somerset* (2001.)

Mills, A.D. *Oxford dictionary of English place names* (Oxford University Press, 1998.)

Millett, M. *Roman Britain* (1995.)

Millett, M. *The Romanisation of Britain* (Cambridge University Press, 1990.)

'Mining Operations of the Romans', in *Proceedings of the Somerset Archaeological and Natural History Society*, vol.VIII (1858), pp.16-18.

Neale, F. 'The site of the Roman villa at Havyatt, Somerset', in *Proceedings of the University of Bristol Spelaeological Society,* vol.12, no.2 (1970), pp.195-202.

North Somerset Landscape Character Assessment (NSCC). Accessed: October, 2004. Electronic source:

http://www.n-somerset.gov.uk/living/planning/policy/

Page, W. (ed). *The Victoria history of the county of Somerset*, Vol.I (1906), pp.306–309.

Perring, D. *The Roman house in Britain* (Routledge, 2002.)

Quinn, P. *Holy wells of Bristol & Bath region*, (Cromwell Press, 1999.)

Rahtz. P.A., & Greenfield, E. *Excavations at Chew Valley Lake, Somerset*. Department of the Environment archaeological reports, no. 8. (HMSO, 1977.)

Scullard, H.H. *Roman Britain: outpost of the empire* (Thames & Hudson, 1979.)

Skinner, J. British Museum, Additional Manuscripts MS 33673. (1818-1824.)

Todd, M. *Studies in the Romano-British villa* (Leicester University Press, 1978.)

Williams, R.G.J. 'The Stratford Lane Roman road and other early routes on Mendip', in *Proceedings of the University of Bristol Spelaeological Society*, vol XIX (1992), pp.151-82.

Wilson, R. *Roman forts: an illustrated introduction to the garrison posts of Roman Britain* (Bergstrom & Boyle, 1980.)

The Creation of the Ecclesiastical Parish known as Blagdon with Charterhouse on Mendip.

Andy Littlejones

On November 6th 1912 the Archbishop of Canterbury, Randall Thomas, signed off a scheme to be presented to His Majesty the King in Council, which would correct an anomaly that had existed for over 700 years. It would bring about the joining together of the Rectory and Parish Church of Blagdon with the Liberty and Extra-Parochial Place known as Charterhouse-on-Mendip which still belonged to the Perpetual Curacy of Witham over 20 miles away. Under the rules of section 26 of the Pluralities Act of 1838, *'the said Liberty may be advantageously separated from Witham and be united and annexed to the said Rectory and Parish Church of Blagdon for Ecclesiastical purposes.'*

The scheme had been submitted to the Archbishop by the Right Reverend George Wyndham, Lord Bishop of Bath and Wells.

His submission states that:

'We George Wyndham Lord Bishop of Bath and Wells do hereby represent to your Grace that there are in the County of Somerset and Diocese of Bath and Wells the Rectory and Parish Church of Blagdon and the Liberty or extra-Parochial Place of Charterhouse on Mendip anciently belonging to Witham Friary.'

'That the annual Income of the said Benefice of Blagdon is about three hundred and seventy-eight pounds Gross and according to the last Census the population thereof was Nine hundred and fifty.'

'That according to the last Census the population of the said Liberty of Charterhouse was 64 living within the boundaries being clearly defined on the said Ordnance Map.'

'That the said Liberty of Charterhouse on Mendip was formerly a monastic foundation and in proof of this there exists the Charter which confirmed the grant made by King Henry II, out of his Royal Manor of Cheddar to the Carthusian House at Witham Friary. The grant was made about the year 1181, together with exemption by the then Bishop from Tithes and all

ecclesiastical dues, and continued in force until the dissolution of the Monasteries. Since then the people residing there have been practically left without the means of Grace until the year 1893 when a fund was raised to provide a stipend for a Clergyman to serve the said Liberty of Charterhouse on Mendip. This fund has continued up to the present time and has been raised entirely by voluntary contributions.'

'That the said Liberty of Charterhouse on Mendip is distant over twenty miles from the Parish of Witham Friary and has never within modern times been served by that Parish the distance rendering it practically impossible.'

'That Baptisms, Marriages and Burials of persons residing in the said Liberty of Charterhouse on Mendip up to the year 1808 were solemnized and performed in the Parish Church of Cheddar and since that date up to the present time have been solemnized and performed in the Parish Church of Blagdon and only one or two isolated cases are known of the ceremonies being performed at Witham Friary.'

'That the said Liberty of Charterhouse on Mendip is contiguous to the said Parish of Blagdon with which it is much intermixed and the inhabitants thereof could be more easily visited by the Rector of Blagdon than by the Vicar of Witham Friary or by the incumbent of any of the neighbouring Parishes.'

'That the Patronage of the said Rectory of Blagdon is vested in George Alfred Wills of Burwalls, Leigh Woods, Clifton, Bristol, Esquire and the Patronage of the Perpetual Curacy of Witham Friary aforesaid is vested in the Duke of Somerset.'

'That it appears to us that under the provisions of the Pluralities Act 1838 the said Liberty of Charterhouse on Mendip so far as it may form part of the said Perpetual Curacy of Witham Friary or of any other Parish than that of Blagdon may be advantageously separated therefrom and be united and annexed to the said Rectory and Parish Church of Blagdon for ecclesiastical purposes.'

As well as that of the Bishop the document has four other signatures which were vital for consents to give the plan authority.

1) George Alfred Wills, of Burwalls, Leigh Woods, Clifton, Bristol, who was the Patron or person entitled to present to the Rectory of Blagdon in the County of Somerset and Diocese of Bath and Wells. He had signed on October 10th 1912.

2) Algernon St Maur, Duke of Somerset, was the Patron or person entitled to present to the Perpetual Curacy of Witham Friary in the County of Somerset and Diocese of Bath and Wells.

3) The Reverend George Menzies Lambrick, Rector of the Parish and Parish Church of Blagdon (Fig 1).

4) The Reverend Percival William Rouse, Incumbent of the Perpetual Curacy of Witham Friary.

The motivation for the union of Blagdon and Charterhouse was to correct an anomaly which was still quite common at the beginning of the 20th century and reflected the days when the great monastic houses of England had been given, or themselves obtained, various lands which were not necessarily contiguous or part of the mother church. This gave rise to two situations, which by the 19th century were increasingly being called into question.

1) Pluralism, which was the simultaneous holding of more than one ecclesiastical benefice. This had been forbidden by statute in 1529, at the time of the dissolution, but had remained common and even increased in the 18th century.

2) Non-residence, which was the holding of a benefice by an absentee clergyman. This had been opposed strongly by the Puritan opposition at the time of the Civil War and under Cromwell up to 1660, but became rife again in the 18th century. By 1810 over half of all clergymen in the Church of England were non-resident.

This state of affairs was not satisfactory to the more disciplined attitude of the Victorians and, following a report of the Ecclesiastical Commissioners in 1836, a permanent commission was established to bring about reform.

The statutory outcome was the Pluralities Act of 1838. Section 26 recognises both of the above situations and goes on to suggest that a correction should be made where appropriate. The Act states that, '*Whereas in some instances Tithings, Hamlets, Chapelries, and other places or Districts may be separated from the Parishes or Mother Churches to which they belong, with advantage; Places altogether Extra-Parochial may, in other instances, **with advantage be annexed to Parishes or Diocese with which they are contiguous**, or be constituted separate Parishes for Ecclesiastical purposes.*'

There were economic and practical advantages as the Act went on to say that, '*changes consequent on such alteration in respect to Ecclesiastical Jurisdiction, Glebe Lands, Tithes, Rent Charges and other Ecclesiastical Dues, Rates and Payments, and in respect to Patronage and Rights to Pews, may be made with justice to all Parties interested.*'

The Blagdon proposal elaborated on this, stating, '*That all fees and ecclesiastical dues and payments for Churchings, Marriages, Burials and ecclesiastical offices solemnized and performed within the said Liberty or District of Charterhouse on Mendip shall belong to the Incumbent and Church Officers of the Parish of Blagdon with Charterhouse on Mendip*'. It finally concluded '*That the Owners and Occupiers of lands and hereditaments in the said Liberty or District of Charterhouse on Mendip shall be entitled in common with the Parishioners of Blagdon to accommodation in the Church of Blagdon but shall not hereafter be entitled to accommodation in the Parish Church of Witham Friary or any other Church than that of Blagdon.*'

The Proposal was successful, as the document concludes, '*NOW, THEREFORE, His Majesty in Council, by and with the advice of His said Council, is pleased to order, as it is hereby ordered, that the said Scheme be carried into effect. Almeria FitzRoy*'

The timing of the union of Blagdon and Charterhouse was almost certainly due to the Rector of Blagdon, George Menzies Lambrick (Fig 1), who, prior to his appointment to Blagdon, had been working as a curate for the Rector of Cheddar

Figure 1 - George Menzies Lambrick Rector of Blagdon 1908-1929

with responsibility for Charterhouse. The problems that the inhabitants of Charterhouse experienced in attending public worship had already been recognised by the Bishop's staff, and from 1894 church services had been held in their local school. Children were baptised there and their names can be found recorded on a small font in St Hugh's church. When Lambrick arrived in Cheddar in 1898 he eagerly took on the task of serving Charterhouse and in the registers he is described as "Mission Curate, Charterhouse on Mendip". It is said that after taking the service at the school on Sundays he would continue on to Blagdon to visit the Court where lived his in-laws, Captain Nathaniel Newnham and his wife Louisa. Lambrick was already well known in Blagdon since his marriage to the Newnhams' daughter Mary Louisa.

When, in 1908, Bishop Kennion offered him the living of Blagdon, Lambrick insisted that the Charterhouse duty was transferred to Blagdon. The bishop agreed and a year later the newly established church of St Hugh was consecrated and services moved there from the school. The rebuilding of the church (Fig 2) was finally completed by the architect W.D. Caroe in 1913, which neatly coincided with the approval of the submitted scheme and the ensuing Order in Council which joined Charterhouse ecclesiastically to Blagdon and renamed the parish Blagdon-with-Charterhouse.

Figure 2 - St Hugh's Church at Charterhouse-on-Mendip

Thus ended an extraordinary situation, which had existed for well over 700 years. But just how did this remote, windswept, inhospitable piece of land become a separate estate with its own rights and freedoms? Why did Charterhouse come under the ecclesiastical authority of Witham, a tiny village some 20 miles away? From where did the name Charterhouse come and why was the church (Fig 2), established only in 1908, consecrated to St Hugh, a Burgundian from the Alpine region of France who had died in 1200?

For the answers to these questions you have to look back to medieval England, to the reign of Henry II and to events that shook the very political and ecclesiastical fabric of the country.

By 1170 it was well known that the relationship between King Henry II and his Archbishop of Canterbury, Thomas à Becket, was not good and the argument about the conflicting powers and rights of the church and state had reached an impasse. At a council at Clarendon on January 13th 1164, Henry had set forth sixteen written articles of law, the so-called Constitutions of Clarendon, which he claimed represented the customs of the realm in relation to the church and which affected church privileges, especially the benefit of clergy (immunity of clergy to prosecution in lay courts). The King wanted Thomas and his fellow bishops to accept these articles, but Thomas, although he at first acquiesced, later repudiated them as contrary to the customs of canon law.

Deeply angered, the king determined to break Thomas, and charged him with various offences. Thomas fled the court and, disguised, made his way circuitously to France, to begin an exile of over six years, while the conflict between archbishop and king divided much of the Western world.

At last, under threat of papal sanctions, Henry and Thomas agreed to a reconciliation of sorts, and on November 3rd 1170 Thomas returned to England. However, when he excommunicated some of the King's bishops and barons, Henry raged against this "low-born clerk". Four of the King's men, acting on their own accord, journeyed to Canterbury and, in his own cathedral, murdered Thomas on December 29th 1170. Thomas à Becket became a martyr, and after miracles were said to have been worked at his tomb, he was canonized by Pope Alexander III in February 1173. Pilgrims began to visit Canterbury in such numbers that it became one of the three most popular Christian shrines in Europe.

Because of the public nature of the argument Henry found himself suspected of involvement in the murder and, under threat of excommunication, he agreed to a number of penances. One of these was to found several religious houses, the first of which was to be Witham Priory near Selwood Forest in Somerset.

The King gave the Royal Manor of Witham to the Carthusian order, which was very strict and austere. The order had been founded by St Bruno in 1084, at La Grande Chartreuse in Dauphine, Burgundy. The Witham grant included land, woods and fishponds and was situated remotely to suit the nature of the Carthusians, who desired solitude. Witham was, however, close to two Roman roads. One was the Fosse Way and the other linked the Channel ports of the south coast to the Mendip lead mines, thus making sense of the inclusion in the grant of the area we now call Charterhouse (although in 1170 that was not how it was known.)

The early years of the new Witham foundation were difficult and it faced much hostility from local people who feared the monks would take away their land. The first two Priors found this hostile environment impossible and it was only with the arrival of the third Prior, Hugh of Avalon, in 1179, that the difficulties were overcome and the mother house of the Carthusian order in England was firmly established.

Hugh found Witham in a state of destitution. There were no proper buildings, the former inhabitants were still in occupation and there were no plans for future development. He was a very different character to his predecessors and already had a reputation for organisation and leadership, which he had achieved at the Carthusian monastery of La Grande Chartreuse near Grenoble. He was able to go to Henry with demands that the King was persuaded to accept.

An offer was made to the occupants of the dwellings to compensate them for losing their homes and to release them from serfdom, and most of them moved to Knapp in North Curry, 30 miles away. After some delay and more deputations to the King, Hugh received the money he needed – the receipt entries in the Pipe Roll of 1179-1188 showed this totalled £672 5s 1d. This was on top of the initial endowment of land that was a generous 5,000 acres. In addition the Carthusian lands were exempted from taxes and taken out of the jurisdiction of the forest officers, thus creating the Liberty referred to in the 1912 document.

So between 1179 and 1188 Hugh changed Witham from virtual destitution to a successful working operation with the completion of the buildings and the creation of a reputation which was already attracting monks from far and wide.

All this resulted in a more detailed charter (Fig 3), which, amongst other things, defined in minute detail the boundaries of the new foundation. Included was the land on West Mendip that was granted for pasture and the establishment of a grange, corresponding roughly with the area we now know as Charterhouse-on-Mendip. The boundaries consisted of a long list of landmarks, notably burial mounds, large rocks, trackways and valleys, that are described in Latin in the foundation charter. Fortunately a great deal of scholarly work has gone into locating these landmarks and we are particularly indebted to the great Mendip historian J.W. Gough and, more recently, to a useful update by our North Somerset archaeologist Vince Russett who was able to utilise details of perambulations and other documents not available to Gough to further fix specific points. The eastern boundary is in line with the present Charterhouse but the west is not so clear and it is likely that Tynings and Milkway were later additions.

It is not known exactly when the name Charterhouse was introduced. There is no separate appearance in Domesday as this area was Royal Forest – Crown property and therefore not assessed for taxes. In the years from 1158 to 1170 there are many entries in the Pipe Rolls referring to Chedderford (also Ceddreford and Ceddrefeld). It was held by Hugh de Gundeville from the King and commanded an annual rent of 40/-. The Carthusian foundation document speaks of the pastures at Cheddarford

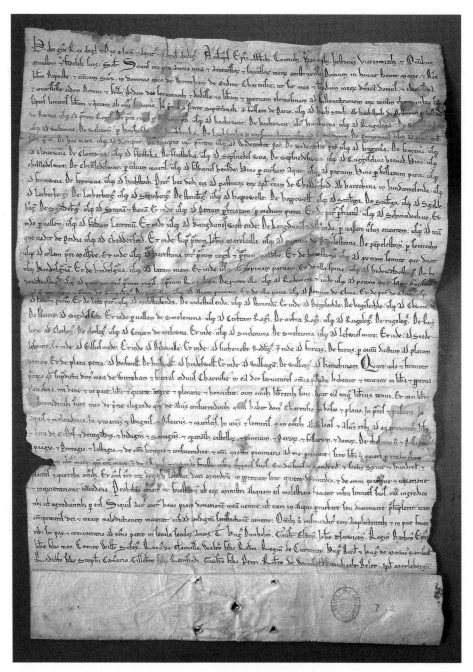

*Figure 3 - The Charter of 1182 in which Henry II granted the lands
at Witham and Charterhouse to the Carthusians.*

(Wells Cathedral Archives ADD/9, photograph by Richard Neale)

and the boundary definition utilises the way leading from Priddy to Cheddarford. By 1183 the Pipe Rolls state that the Brothers of Witham hold Cedreford from the King and more entries between 1185 and 1189 confirm this. It is safe to assume that by the end of the reign of Henry II the situation had stabilised and the Carthusians were recognised as the owners and in place as the occupants.

The succeeding reigns of Henry's sons Richard and John were very eventful for all the wrong reasons but it is significant to note that Hugh had made such an impact as Prior of Witham that in 1186 he was elected Bishop of Lincoln, which he initially refused but then reluctantly accepted after an order from Jancelin, prior of the Grande Chartreuse. The Carthusian order is the most austere and solitary in the Christian church and Hugh was the only Carthusian monk ever to be a bishop of an English diocese. In 1186 Lincoln was a large town of 8,000 people, its diocese the largest in England, comprising nine counties from the Humber to the Thames. So, next to the archbishops, the Bishop of Lincoln represented the most powerful ecclesiastical position in the realm. In 12th century England many bishops were royal officials immersed in secular business, and for the remaining fourteen years of his life Hugh had the confidence of the sovereign, spending much of his time at the royal court. Indeed, during the long absences at the crusades of King Richard, Hugh virtually ran the country, and when he died in London in 1200 a great funeral was held, the coffin taking six days to travel to Lincoln, watched all the way by vast crowds. The mass was attended by three archbishops, fourteen bishops and 100 heads of monastic houses, and the party which carried Hugh's coffin into Lincoln Cathedral included two kings, John of England and William of Scotland.

Hugh's achievements at Lincoln and at court are well known, as there is much information about him thanks to the monk, Adam, who was later abbot of Eynsham. He was a contemporary of Hugh, having much personal contact with him, and his detailed work, the *Magna vita hugonis*, was completed in 1213 as part of the preparations for Hugh's canonisation. From this we can establish that Hugh had sufficient power and influence in high places to keep a watching eye over his passion, the Priory at Witham. Adam tells us that Hugh visited Witham every year until his death and saw it as a place for peaceful relaxation and meditation. With such a patron Witham was bound to prosper.

In 1229 Henry III confirmed the grant of the foundation charter and the same king in 1250 reconfirmed again referring to the lands of the "new Chartreuse on Menedeep".

Here we see the first mention of the new name and, although Cedderford is still occasionally used in later documents, Chartreuse became recognised, evolving into Charterhouse. Thus the origin of today's name is not the "Charter" but Chartreuse, the place in Burgundy where the first Carthusian monastery was established.

The 1250 document also states that the prior and brethren of the new Chartreuse on Menedeep were "exempt from regard of the forest", maintaining the freedom from financial burdens and legal restrictions which were applicable to other landholders. Thus Charterhouse became known as the Liberty, as referred to in the 1912 proposal, which indicates that this status was, from an ecclesiastical standpoint, still accepted.

There has been much debate amongst historians as to whether the site at Charterhouse-on-Mendip contained a religious house with practising Carthusian monks. The foundation charter says nothing about a monastery or a cell and speaks only of pastures at Cheddarford, as do the Pipe Rolls. A monastic cell could however have been installed later and, as we have seen, the patent rolls of 1250 do refer to the land of the prior and brethren of the new Carthusian house on Mendip. However there is no conclusive evidence and the current thinking is still that this refers to the monks at Witham and that Charterhouse remained just a grange, a centre for pasture and an economic unit of the main priory. It was manned by local labourers and supervised by lay brothers living in substantial single storey buildings on the sites of Lower or Manor farms – probably both. In addition, in 1282 Edward I conceded that whatever lead mines the brothers found on their land they might work and use the profit as they thought best. So they were in the lead business as well as sheep and we must assume that the Carthusians were important to the West Minery, which had centred on this area since before the Romans and was to continue to produce lead until the late 19th century. We can conclude that the Roman road, which passed close to Witham and led to Charterhouse, would have been a very important link between the mother house and one of its main sources of wealth. More evidence comes from the *Valor ecclesiasticus*, drawn up as a prelude to the dissolution of the monasteries, which inspected monastic revenues for Henry VIII. This gave no hint of a religious community and referred to Charterhouse as one of the Witham estates.

This relationship is consistent with that of the other Somerset Carthusian monastery at Hinton Charterhouse and its grange on Mendip at Green Ore where sheep and lead were also the main concerns. Both of these Carthusian houses were treated in a similar way by the King. A patent of Edward II in 1309 relieved the monks of Witham and Hinton from taxation of their spiritual and temporal goods, and in 1318 another patent by the same monarch stated that both Somerset Charterhouses were to be free of any Papal levy that should be laid on England.

Thus the Carthusians remained at Charterhouse for some 360 years, apparently in peace and prosperity. Most documentary references refer either to reconfirmation of the original charter, particularly the freedom from taxation on their spiritual and temporal goods, or to the occasional territorial dispute with the Bishop of Wells to the south-east and the men of Cheddar to the west. Sometime during the time of the Carthusians the name Hydon (Hidun) became firmly linked with Charterhouse and we see many references to Charterhouse-Hydon, the name lasting until well after the dissolution. Gough argues that Hidun predates the Carthusians and refers to a location within the area allocated by the 1182 charter.

This period of relative stability was ended by the Reformation and the dissolution of the monasteries which followed Henry VIII's break with Rome in the 1530s. Much of the suppression was of a violent nature as in the case of nearby Glastonbury where Abbott Whyting, who resisted the King's orders, was dragged to the Tor and hanged with two fellow monks. His body was mutilated, his head placed on a pole over the gateway and the Abbey buildings destroyed. Maybe because of such examples the monks of Witham chose to go quietly. Their suppression document was signed by the Prior and twelve monks and each of them received a pension. Three of the monks were still recipients fourteen years later and one of them, a Thurston Hyckmans, was to join the revived Sheen monastery under Mary Tudor and died as a Carthusian at Bruges in 1575.

After the dissolution, the monastic lands were either taken into the new Church of England, as in the case of St Augustine's Abbey which became Bristol Cathedral, or were given or sold to the laity. At Witham the bulk of the monastic estate was granted to Ralph Hopton. The lay brothers' chapel continued as the parish church (Fig 4) in the new Church of England and the patron (Hopton) could appoint and dismiss the curate. However the various lords of the manor took very little interest in the church so it survived almost untouched into the 19th century as a beautiful Norman building. The incumbent did not have a residence or adequate stipend (as before 1827 it was only £40 per year), so Witham had to be held with some other living and as a result was neglected.

At Charterhouse in September 1544, Robert May received the '*grant in fee of the manor or Grange of Hydon in the tenure of Ralph Hopton, formerly belonging to Witham*' and the May family remained lords of the manor for over 100 years. Whether the May family actually lived in Charterhouse or just let out the buildings and land is not certain, although the two houses at Manor Farm and Lower Farm saw considerable rebuilding and enlargement during the 16th and 17th centuries. The coat of arms over the large doorway at Lower Farm is almost certainly that of the May family. The gold chevron between three roses argent had been granted to Robert May in 1573 and his son John was Sheriff of Somerset in 1600. So for a time the family held considerable local power and influence.

Figure 4 - The Parish Church at Witham Friary,
once the Carthusian Church of the Lay Brothers.

In 1660, heavily in debt, the May family sold out to the Gores of Barrow Gurney, and for the following century there are frequent records showing the leases and inventories drawn up between the Gore family and the many tenants who occupied the houses and farms of Charterhouse. The Gores may have used Charterhouse as a summer residence. A date of 1694 on the chimney at Manor Farm indicates an enlargement of the building at that time.

In 1750 William Gore (1701-69) passed the estate to his cousin John Gore of Flax Bourton, and it was John who sold Charterhouse in 1751 to Welbore Ellis, created first Baron Mendip in 1794. In 1761 Ellis drew up one of the most useful estate maps of Charterhouse, showing all the field names and listing the tenants with details of their holdings. The son of the Bishop of Meath, Welbore Ellis died in 1802, and the estate then passed to his grand-nephew, Henry Welbore, 2nd Viscount Clifden, who took the additional name of Ellis. In 1861 Charterhouse school opened on land donated by Lord Clifden. His son George James Welbore was Baron Dover.

In 1884 Charterhouse was given to Henry's niece, the Hon. Lilah Georgina Augusta Constance Agar Ellis, on her marriage to Sir Luke White, Baron Annaly. By then the estate was being managed by trustees. During Lady Annaly's ownership Piney Sleight and some small properties were added and she gave the site for St Hugh's Church. The Edwardian period (1901–10) saw a long depression in agriculture causing reduced rents and leading to an increasing number of farms coming up for sale. At Charterhouse a major sell-off of the various farms and land took place just after the First World War, and produced the pattern of owner occupation that we see today. One anomaly was that the mineral rights in Velvet Bottom were retained by the Clifden Estates up until 1925.

Thus from a civil point of view Charterhouse developed, after the dissolution of the monasteries, in line with the rest of the country. Although it was still referred to as the Liberty, in 1827 the Parish of Charterhouse merged into Blagdon in the Archdeaconry of Wells and on practical issues like the censuses, which began in 1841, it was treated as a part of Blagdon. When the school opened it was seen very much as linked with Blagdon and the school log records the fact that for many years the Rector of Blagdon, the Reverend Gilbert Lyons, was chairman of the school board and eminent Blagdonians like Captain and Mrs Newnham and Mr W.H. Wills visited and took a great interest in the school.

From the ecclesiastical standpoint it was different and the historic alignment between Witham and Charterhouse survived long after the dissolution. The parishes of Cheddar and then Blagdon fulfilled the practical ecclesiastical needs of the Charterhouse inhabitants but it was only with the petition of 1912 that the parish of 'Blagdon with Charterhouse' was formally created and the break with Witham made final. Today Witham Priory exists only as a few humps and bumps in a field dissected by a railway line, although the lay brothers' church (Fig 4) remains as the Witham parish church and keeps much of the character and features that date back to the time of the Carthusian foundation. As we have seen, Charterhouse did not have its own separate church building until 1908 and then it took the name of Hugh of Avalon, that Carthusian monk from Burgundy who had died more than 700 years before. There is no evidence that Hugh ever visited Charterhouse, let alone lived there, but I am sure that he would be pleased that his memory has been preserved in this delightful building in a remote corner of Mendip where for many centuries the strict rules of his Carthusian order held sway.

The full text of the document proposing the union of Blagdon with Charterhouse along with the Royal approval is available in the Somerset Record Office at Taunton.

Bibliography:

Low, *Charterhouse on Mendip*, Chapter 2, 'The Carthusians on Mendip'.

E. Margaret Thompson, *History of the Somerset Carthusians* (1896).

Michael McGarvie, *Witham Friary: church and parish*, (Frome Society for Local Study, 1981.)

Aiden Bellenger, "The Carthusians of Somerset", in *South Western Catholic history*, 2003.

Burrow, "Witham Priory: the first English Carthusian monastery:1965 excavations by Barlow & Reid" in *Proceedings of the SANHS*, 1990

Basil Fletcher & Robert Dunning, *Saint Hugh of Witham and his Priory* (Bath & West Diocesan Board)

David Farmer, *Saint Hugh of Lincoln* (Bath & West Diocesan Board, 1985)

St Hugh's (The Mendip Society.)

Burgess, *Charterhouse: the story so far* (Axbridge History Society, 1989.)

Gough, "Witham Carthusians on Mendip" in *Proceedings of the SANHS*, 1928.

F.A. Knight, *The heart of Mendip* (1915), chapter on Charterhouse.

Frances Neale, *Mendip: a new study*, ed. Robin Athill (1976), chapter 4.

Russett, "An enigma in retreat", in *CHERT proceedings*, vol 1

History of the County of Somerset (Victoria County History, 1911), vol. II, pp.123–128.

Carthusian Foundation charter with bounds (Wells Cathedral Library.)

1761 map of Charterhouse, Somerset Record Office DD/STL1.

Particulars of rents and accounts of Gore family, Somerset Record Office DD/ BR/1ch 1.

DIBBINS'S TO POST OFFICE STORES

Olga Shotton

The record of a group of deeds at Somerset Record Office led to further investigations concerning the history of a piece of land which fronts the High Street in Blagdon and is bounded on the other three sides by Mead Lane, the Mead and Bath Road.

The Redwood family, who once ran the village shop, as many older residents will remember, had deposited the deeds, but when the shop changed hands the deeds were withdrawn from the S.R.O. and now seem to have disappeared. Luckily, a précis of the contents was made and is now accessible. The following account was stimulated initially by the deeds, and by transcripts of further material from Somerset Record Office now held in the Blagdon Local History Society archive.

In 1711, and possibly for some years earlier, Henry Gorges, the lord of the manor of Blagdon, had leased the piece of land with which we are presently concerned to members of the Dibbins family. A steward or reeve administered the land for the lord of the manor, since a wealthy landowner would have had many such manors. Regular 'Courts Baron', held in each manor, were attended by all those who held land from the lord. Non-attendance was fined. A group of tenants was elected to hear and judge any complaints and to settle the amount of any fines levied, for instance for not keeping ditches clear, for encroaching on someone else's land, or for failing to perform any duties due to the lord. A written record of this court was kept, but in the case of Blagdon has not survived for this period. The records were written on sheets of parchment. Each sheet was then sewn to the previous sheet and the whole record rolled up – hence 'court roll'. As the reeve or steward was often responsible for a number of manors, this was a convenient way to carry the records.

Those who worked land belonging to a manor normally held their plots by 'copy of court roll', that is, the transaction was entered in the steward's record, and a copy was made and given to the tenant. This agreement often contained conditions, so that besides the rent of the property, the tenant might have to plough a certain area of the lord's land, or perhaps provide labour for the lord's haymaking, provide produce for the lord's table, or other work. Upon the death of the tenant, a fee called a heriot was due to the lord, usually the best beast or best possession. If a son wished to take over the land, a levy called an entry fine had to be paid. An arrangement that became common later was a lease for 99 years or three lives. The three people whose lives were part of the lease were named, and their ages noted. Frequently the man, his wife and his son were cited in the document. When all three people had died, the land reverted to the lord of the manor. Examples of these two types of tenancy can be seen in the Aldwick records in the Blagdon archive at Court Lodge.

Beside the commitment to the civil authority, a rate was paid to the church, based on the acreage owned, rented or leased. This originated in the 13th century as a voluntary payment toward the upkeep of the fabric of the church, but by the 18th century had become compulsory. The yearly payments, decided by the Vestry (comprising the Rector, the churchwardens and overseers, and several parishioners), were entered in the churchwardens' accounts. The amount of the rate had to be ratified by the Bishop. Although the churchwardens' accounts for Blagdon have survived from 1599 forward, there is a gap from 1662 to 1698, when it appears that a whole book of accounts has been lost, probably in the turbulent times after the Civil War, and the later religious controversies. The Dibbins family, therefore, may have held land earlier than 1711, but there are no records to verify this.

'Dibbins' occupies two acres, originally arranged as two long strips, north to south. An ox-team and plough could plough an acre in a working day, and since the plough was cumbersome to turn, it was sensible to make the furrows lengthwise of the plot. (*Fig 1*) The remains of this arrangement can be seen to this day.

Fig 1 Ploughing with an ox-team, from Pyne's Microcosm, 1802

The spelling of the clerk who kept the churchwardens' accounts was often erratic. The entry in 1711 and for the next few years is as follows:-

1711 Robert dibins for boath	*5/1*
1711 Richard dibing	*4/9*
1712 Late Robert Dibbins	*2/6*
1712 Richard Dibbins	*3/2*
1713 Late Robert Dibbins for both	*2/6*
1714 Richard Dibbins	*3/2*
1714 Late Robert Dibbins for both	*3/4*

Records of sales of land sometimes had a note of previous changes of ownership added at the bottom of the sheet, called a recitation; the first of the deeds about 'Dibbins', although recording a sale of the land in 1793, has such an addendum, which gives some useful information.

Henry Gorges, the lord of the manor of Blagdon, died in 1717, and was succeeded by his son Robert, who sold 'Dibbins's' to John Brookman, who held it until his death in 1742, when he willed it to Thomas Ozen. The Dibbins family still rented the land, and continued to pay the church rate.

1718 Richard Dibbins	*4/9*
1718 Late Robert Dibbins for both	*5/0½*
1719 Richard Dibbins	*3/2*
1719 Late Robert Dibbins	*1/5*
1737 Mr Dibbens	*6/4*
1738 Sam'l Dibbins	*2/2*
1739 Sam'l Dibbins	*6/9*
1742 Sam'l Dibbins	*6/4*
1748 Sam'l Dibbens	*3/2*

The variation in payments was because the church rate, which was set by the Vestry members each year, altered according to need. For example the high rate in 1739 and 1742 may have been to fund repairs to the gallery in the church mentioned in the churchwardens accounts.

1751 Samuel Dibbins	*3/2*
1754 Samuel Dibbins	*6/4*

In 1756 Thomas Ozen and his wife Frances sold the land to William Foord, but the Dibbins family continued as tenants.

1759 Richard Dibbins	*6/4*		
1760 Richard Dibbins	*3/2*		
1763 Richard Dibbins	*3/2*	*and Mrs Plaister*	*6/4*

The Plaister family held land in what is now the Station Road area and in Butcombe, and one Richard Dibbins of Butcombe, aged 74, was buried in Blagdon in 1797. He would have been 40 years old in 1763. There is no record of change of use of 'Dibbins's', but it may be that an orchard was planted in part of it at this time. This use of the land may mean that houses of a simple sort were also erected, and the land seems to have been shared with others for the next few years.

| 1764 Richard Dibbins | 3/2 | and Benjamin Williams | 6/4 |
| 1766 Richard Dibbins | 2/1 | and George Williams | 4/3 |

The tenure of the Dibbins family is coming to an end. During the next few years rates seem to be paid, but the reference is to 'the late' and the rate is low.

1766 Late Samuel Dibbins	1/0½
1767 Late Richard Dibbins	1/0½
1769 Late Samuel Dibbins	1/0½
1770 Late Richard Dibbins	1/0½

In the year 1770 Samuel Dibbins 'of Broadfield Down' was buried in Blagdon, and Richard Dibbins 'of Butcombe' died in 1797 at the age of 74. Perhaps Richard had been unable for some years to manage the land. This ends the 60 year association of the Dibbins family with the land. No rate appears to have been paid for 1771-1772, but in 1773 the use of the land was shared between John Patch and John Sommers Esq.

1773-4 John Patch	2/1	and John Sommers, Esq.
1775-6 John Patch	2/1	and John Sommers, Esq
1779 John Sommers, Esq	4/3	and John Patch for late Dibbins's 2/-

In 1784 a rate was paid for Valentine Dudden's orchard of 1 rood 23 perches. Valentine Dudden will appear again, so perhaps this is the orchard planted on Dibbin's.

| 1787 John Sommers Esq 4/3 | and -----Hoock 2/2 |

In 1789 William Foord died, and is said to have left land to his son Samuel Foord. William Foord's will was proved at Wells in 1790, and a copy exists at the Somerset Record Office but it mentions only William's sons William and James and his daughter Jane. Nor is there any reference to 'Dibbins', though William held several plots of land in the parish. William mentions a relative called William Foord in his will who was a butcher in Blagdon, but if the will of this second William Foord exists it has not come to light, so that we do not know if this second William was the one who had a son Samuel, and who was the William to whom the land was left.

The first of the deeds mentioned at the beginning of this article is dated 1793, when Isaac Sperrin of Blagdon sold Dibbins's to Edward Gallop. The plot is described as 'a messuage and orchard, with a cider mill and press thereon, formerly parcel of the manor'. The cider-making equipment would be likely to be under cover, and 'messuage' usually describes living accommodation, but it is not possible to say in what part of the plot this building was situated.

Edward Gallop obtained the land on 14th October and the next day mortgaged it to Richard Panes.

Another part of the land was covered by a mortgage granted by widow Susanna Marshall of Cheddar in 1791. The mortgage was sold on to William Lewkins of Cheddar in 1792 and thence to Isaac Sperrin(g). Widows who had been left money by their husbands often lent it out at interest in mortgages as an investment.

Meanwhile those who were living on the land still paid their church rate.

1804   John Patch, part of Dibbens 4/3
*   Robert Phippen, part of Dibbens 2/2*

In April 1806 Edward Gallop seems to have sold part of Dibbens's to Richard Derrick, schoolmaster, of Blagdon, who also would have taken over the mortgage, but in May 1806 butcher John Lawrence purchased part of the land. It will soon be possible to more precise about his purchase. Valentine Dudden appears again in 1810. It may be that the orchard, cider mill and press belonged to him.

1810 Church Rates: Robert Phippens part Dibbins 9d,
*   Valentine Dudden part Dibbins 1/5*

The next deed mentions a shopkeeper. It seems that a shop, if not already trading, would shortly be doing so!

In 1817 John Lawrence sold to James Spear, shopkeeper. The area is defined as bordered on the south-east and west by the new turnpike road. The later tithe map indicates that this was the northernmost part of Dibbins's, probably the site of the present shop. A memorandum attached to the deed mentions that twenty perches of ground were to be reserved to John Lawrence for the erection of a cottage. In the next deed in the series, 1825, James Spear took out a mortgage with James Bennett of Aldwick. After James Bennett's death, his widow transferred the mortgage to John Cox, gentleman, of Wrington.

The church rates after 1821 are not entered in the churchwardens' accounts. A separate book was used which curiously begins in 1841. Perhaps the record was kept in a less permanent form in the intervening years. Unfortunately the rates in the new book do not mention the names of fields, probably because the central part of the parish at least was being built up. Entries are therefore usually for 'Land' or 'House and Garden'. However the entry for 1841 mentions that William Heal had a blacksmith's shop, rateable value £1 15s, and land at £10 15s, and Mr Lawrence had a house and a butchers shop, rateable value £5.

At this point we can turn at last to a more detailed view of the area. The tithe map of 1842-3 shows all the land in the parish and numbers the various fields and plots. A list of the owners and occupiers, a record of land use (such as arable, pasture or woodland) together with a note of the area in acres, roods and perches, and the valuation for rating, make this document extremely valuable to the historian, not least because after this time documents nearly always mention the tithe number of property, so that its position in the parish can be gauged.

It is now possible to see how Dibbins's became divided up (*Fig 2*). The original longitudinal division can still be seen, but development has taken place along the turnpike road edge and along Mead Lane. The original entrance to Blagdon Court was along Mead Lane, the present driveway being made after the turnpike house was demolished, and the semi-circular entrance to the present drive reflects the probable shape of the turnpike keeper's house as depicted on the tithe map.

The building now called Court Lodge was then a cottage fronting the main road, although the surface of the road was much lower, as can be seen from the present position of the back door to Court Lodge, and it must have been a long pull for horses and wagons ascending the road from the Coombe to the Scymour Arms corner. The adverse camber outside Court Lodge still presents difficulties for lorries, as can be seen by the frequent damage to Court Lodge roof and the frontage of the George.

A list of the owners and occupiers of Dibbins's as in Figure 2:-

Owner	Occupier	No	Description	Acreage
Mary Andrews	Mary Andrews	344	Dwelling & Garden	0-0-24
James Panes	William Spurlock	345	House, Shop, Garden	0-1-27
John Cox	William White	346	House, Shop, etc.	0-0-32
William Heale	William Heale	347	Cottage & Garden	0-0-15
Jos. Lawrence	Levi Thomas	348	House & Garden	0-1-6

The record of the acreage is expressed in roods and perches but it does not add up very well. It may be that the area originally extended further into what is now the Mead.

At about this time, in 1841, the first of the more detailed censuses were made, and so it is possible to discover more about the families living on Dibbins's. Censuses had been taken every ten years since 1801, but the great bulk of the evidence collected for the earlier years was destroyed once the statistical tables had been compiled.

William White was a tailor. By looking at successive censuses, it is possible to trace part of his history.

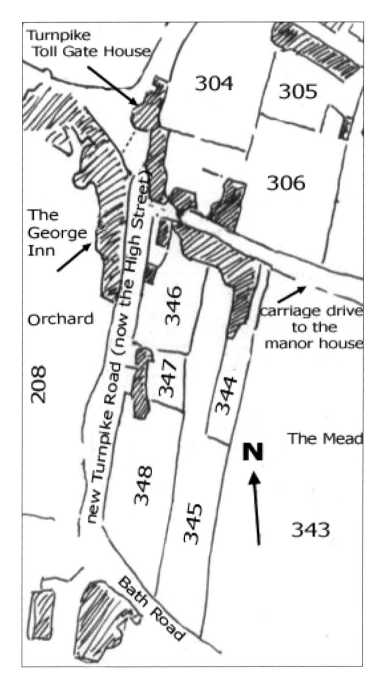

Figure 2 – Extract from the 1842 Tithe Map

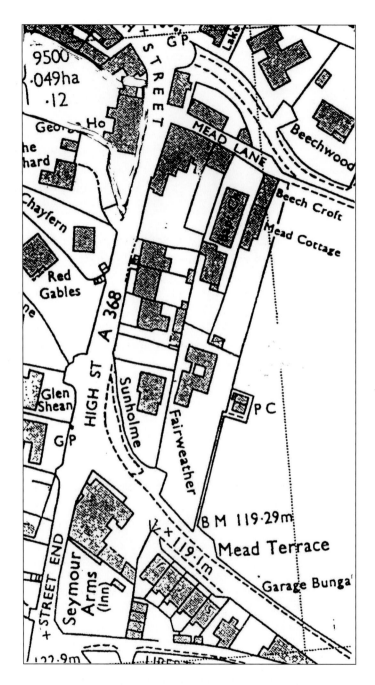

Figure 3 —a more recent map of the area c1931

1841 census

Wm White, tailor, and his wife Diana, both aged 45, together with his mother Elizabeth aged 70, lived where the Post Office Stores now stands. He had three daughters, Ellen, aged 20, Louisa, 18, and Martha, 7, and a son, John, aged 14. His house and shop were rented from, or possibly mortgaged to, John Cox of Wrington.

William Heal, the blacksmith, also aged 45, was the owner of his cottage and garden, living there with his wife Sarah who was 40. They had seven children: Frederick, 25, Ephraim, 20, Simeon, 15, Matilda, 12, Henry, 10, Walter, 8, and Louisa, 5. The blacksmith's shop was further up the High Street, probably where the topmost cottage now stands.

Mary Andrews, aged 60, who owned and lived in one of the cottages now called Mead Cottages, next to the present Mead, is recorded as independent in 1841

Jos. Lawrence, a butcher, aged 60, seems to be a widower, and was living with his family, probably in the cottage which he owned on Dibbins's, and which was mentioned in the deed when he sold part of his holding. He reserved part of the land to build a house for himself. It is likely that that house was Redwood Cottage. Also living in the house were Sydenham, aged 25, who died in 1841, Louisa, 20, Phebe, 20, Mary, 15, who died in 1846, and Edmond, 15. Someone called Ann Heal, aged 20, with her son Henry, aged 1 year, is living in a cottage next door, which was probably removed or was derelict when the Baptist chapel was built. It seems likely that Ann, who is recorded as 'Independent,' was involved with the Lawrence family, and was probably related to William Heal the smith in the High Street.

Levi Thomas may have moved to this house later in the year, after the census but before the tithe apportionment was compiled. Levi was a shoemaker, aged 25, and lived with his wife Sarah also 25, and three young children, Edward, 4, Charles, 2, and Louisa, 6 months old.

William Spurlock, another butcher, is recorded as living on tithe number 345, which had a large piece of land attached to it, which may have been used to keep animals which were to be slaughtered later. However, Sarah Spurlock, aged 65, is recorded in the census as head of the family, and as a butcher, living with her daughter Ann, aged 25, and sons John, 25, and George, aged 20. This is probably the cottage fronting Mead Lane and nearest the present Mead. It is likely that William Spurlock died between the time of the census and the time of the tithe map, a matter of months. William Spurlock's plot belonged to James Panes, and George Panes, aged 20, seems to be living in a house on the same land, perhaps as a lodger or neighbour.

1851 census

Censuses were taken every ten years, recording the people in each house on a certain night. If any of the family were visiting elsewhere they were recorded there, so that we may not have a full record of a family.

William and Diana White seem to have prospered by 1851. He had now become a tailor and draper, employing one man and two apprentices, George and Edwin Harris. There is no mention of his family, but it was common for girls to be employed as servants in better-off families, where they lived in, usually being given clothing and board to supplement small wages.

William Heal's business had grown, so that he employed his son Simeon, now 26, in blacksmithing. His son Ephraim also helped with the business, and had married and had three children. Ephraim and his family also lived with William. Frederick, however, had married and moved elsewhere, and his son Henry, aged 6, happened to be with William on census night.

George Panes, now 36, is recorded as a butcher, and lived with his wife Jane, 34. They had four young children, Louisa, 4, Eliza, 4, Elizabeth, 2, and Edmund, one year old.

Sarah Spurlock is now 73, still a butcher, and only her son George, aged 32, is living with her.

Mary Andrews, at 75, had a granddaughter, Eliza Spencer, aged 12, living with her. (The apparent disparity in her age is because ages in 1841 were often rounded up to the nearest five, to make reckoning of age groups for statistical purposes simpler.) Nearby in Blagdon lived George and Albinia Spencer, both 38, who are probably Eliza's parents. George was a shoemaker. Children often seem to have been living in relatives' houses, possibly because living accommodation was cramped, or to be of help to the aged.

1861 census

Ten years later, both William and Diana White are aged 69, and living on their own. There was no old age pension at this time, so that unless they had considerable savings, or help from their children, they would still have had to work.

William Heal the blacksmith died in 1854, aged 62, Simeon in 1855 aged 31, and Ephraim in 1860 aged 40. Henry Heal is mentioned as a blacksmith, and lives in the same place with his wife Ann and two young children, Sarah aged 2 and William aged one year. Three of Ephraim Heal's children are living together. Susan Heal, now aged 17, is recorded as a shopkeeper, William is a blacksmith, at 15 years old, and Elfleda is 13.

Levi Thomas, recorded as a cordwainer (a leather worker or shoemaker), is now 49, and his wife Sarah is 51. His daughter Susan Pamela, aged 14, is recorded as a needlewoman. The other children are elaborately named John Adolphus, aged 12, William Guilford, aged 10 and Matilda C. aged 5. The older children, Edward and Charles, would be in their teens, and probably apprenticed away from home, but Louisa seems to have disappeared.

Sarah Spurlock died in 1856 aged 79, but George Spurlock her son is working as an agricultural labourer and lives with his wife Elizabeth, recorded as a goosewife.

George Harris, William White's apprentice, now aged 28, has married a wife, Martha, aged 27, and has his wife's sister Emma, aged 17, living with them. Both the ladies are milliners. This family may have lived in Beech Cottage, across Mead Lane, or in Court Lodge, as the next entry in the census return is Blagdon Court.

By 1861 Mary Andrews had moved to a house next to the Wesleyan Methodist chapel (now a private house) in the Bath Road. She was now 85, was living with her 47 year old daughter, Mary Ann, and is described as a retired grocer. As Mary Andrews at first lived in a cottage facing the present football field, she may have run a small shop there.

1871 census
By 1871 the shop has been leased to Albert Taylor, aged 26, and his wife Elizabeth, He is described as a general shopkeeper

William White is now a widower aged 80, and is lodging with George Spurlock the butcher, the son of William Spurlock, who owned a house, shop and garden facing Mead Lane.

The land adjoining the Spurlock house extended the whole length of the 'Dibbins' land. It is probable that the butchery business included keeping animals for at least a short time until they were slaughtered.

Mary Andrews died on her birthday, December 21st, aged 97, in 1868. Her daughter Mary Ann, now aged 54, is recorded as a shopkeeper and beer-house keeper living in the East End.

Andrew's beer-house is mentioned in the churchwardens' accounts of the time as a place where the churchwardens and various tradesmen concluded deals for work on the church, so perhaps it was part of, or on the site of, the New Inn, handily near the church.

John White, the son of William the tailor, died in 1878, aged 66.

1881 census

At the time of the 1881 census, Albert Taylor, now aged 36, and his wife Elizabeth (recorded as a milliner and dressmaker) are still running the shop, and probably a dressmaking business as well. Ann Bath, aged 16, was employed by them as a servant and no doubt helped to look after the three children, Wilfred aged 9, Allun aged 4, and the one month old baby Edith Kate.

George Spurlock, now 60, does not appear to have continued the family business as a butcher and is recorded as a general labourer. His wife Elizabeth, aged 51, however, has styled herself 'schoolmistress' and her daughter as schoolmistress's assistant. This lady seems likely to be the source of another Blagdon legend, that of the schoolmistress with a 'wooden arm' with which she used to belabour errant pupils! In this household also lodged Joseph Gallop, the Parish Clerk, a 95 year old widower.

The village shops have been augmented by Benjamin Panes's Post Office and general stores. Benjamin and his wife Anna Marie, besides the shop business, later did well in property deals. Their two sons and a daughter became missionaries in India, coming back to Blagdon eventually. The shop was opposite the present Rectory, where 'Body & Soul' replaced the Post Office within living memory.

1891 census

By 1891 the family business of Albert Taylor has increased. His son Wilfred is an assistant in the shop and Percy (not present on the previous census) and Allun help out. Edith has been joined by Gertrude, now aged 7, and Theodore Albert, only 2 months old. Also in the shop on census night were two dressmaking assistants, Alice Prior and Margaret Hopkins, both aged 20.

George Spurlock is now 70 years old, and his wife is 64 and no longer a schoolmistress.

At this time, the Baptist congregation was meeting in a room in The Bell, a public house, now gone, in Bell Square. This was not very satisfactory, and funds were raised to construct a proper chapel on the present site, known as the Jubilee Chapel because it was built in Queen Victoria's Jubilee year. This closed the gap between the back of the shop and the cottage next door and the row of cottages beside the football field, and as the site was of some depth from the frontage it was possible to reserve space for a schoolroom and a small garden. This was probably the site of the butchery business, and perhaps some buildings were demolished in order to make the requisite width for the chapel.

By 1901 the shop has changed hands and is run by Edward Green, aged 29, who is also a mason. A married man, his wife Amelia is 30, and his children are Percival, 6, Gertrude, 4, and Bertha, aged one year. Wilfred Taylor, now aged 29, lives nearby with his wife Kate, 22, and is recorded as a grocer's assistant.

In 1906 the shop was bought by the Taylor family, and called 'The Supply Stores'. The Taylors had also developed businesses in Long Ashton (Percy Taylor) and Banwell (Allun Taylor). They took out a mortgage with Thomas Caple, a yeoman of Ubley. Wilfred ran the shop in Blagdon until 1911, when Albert Taylor died. The shop was then sold to the Redwood family from West Harptree.

Many people now living remember 'Redwoods'. The cottage next door was dubbed 'Redwoods Cottage'. The shop employed eight local people and made deliveries in the area. No doubt the variety of goods stocked was greatly increased. Like some other houses in the village, water was not laid on until 1932, and supplies were pumped up from a well in the back yard. Paraffin was sold from a store also in the back yard, as most houses relied on paraffin for lamps, and some also cooked on paraffin-fuelled stoves. Ken Nelson, from the Post Office opposite the present Rectory, kept the accounts. At Christmas, regular customers were given small gifts – a blotter (a necessity in the days of pen and ink) or a small decorative pot to hold matches, or some other trifle. Examples of these two gifts still exist in Blagdon Local History Society's archive, the blotter in good condition still, the little white china pot broken, although it is still possible to see the picture of the Rock of Ages on it, and the inscription underneath 'Redwoods Stores, Blagdon'.

The Redwoods attended the Baptist church, conveniently nearby, and both sons played the organ there. Brian Redwood, the younger son, remembers Mr Parry, the pastor, who lived in the lower part of Street End. Mrs Redwood ran the Women's Bright Hour. When Mr Redwood died his son Charles Collins Redwood took over (fig. 4). He was always known as 'Colin'. The association of the Redwood family with the shop lasted until 1945, when 'Baker' Cole, whose business, first in Gilcombe House, on the corner of Church Street and Bath Road, and then in the house now known as The Old Bakery, bought it in partnership with his son Donald, who had, when younger, helped with deliveries of bread after school. Donald worked in an insurance firm when he left school. Later, during World War II, he was in the Fire Service and became Chief Fire Officer for Burnham. When he returned to Blagdon, he and his father bought the shop as a partnership. Donald was in charge of the shop while his father ran the bakery. This meant that groceries as well as bread could be delivered.

A van chassis was purchased, and a body was built on it in Blagdon. The van had no windscreen – one had to peer over a metal deflector. The early braking system, which depended on a narrow brake shoe, could not hold the van on the steep Mendip hills, and when stopping to make deliveries the front wheels had to be turned into the wall to hold the vehicle. The van had no doors, so to start off again the driver had to wrench the wheels straight and leap in as the van began to move! Further, there were no lights until, after many warnings by the local policeman (probably Mr Boyce), bicycle lamps running on acetylene were fixed to the front. They were no use as headlamps, but enabled other traffic to see the van!

At the present day, there is still the trace of the original "division of Dibbins's, with" a row of houses bordering High Street and another row at the edge of The Mead. One of the High Street houses, once the home of Mary Ann Filer, is now known as Sovereign Cottage, after a locally well known and authentic story about a house fire there, when the occupier, thought to be hard-up, was discovered to have money stored everywhere! Two modern houses occupy the area opposite the Seymour Arms at the southern end of the plot. The Baptist chapel and meeting room, together with the grassed area to the south, probably preserves the shape of the butchers field which held animals due for slaughter. The building of the chapel will be recorded in a later article on the history of non-conformists in Blagdon.

The blacksmith's house and yard was possibly the topmost house in the High Street, where there is a wide passage to the rear premises. It is known that a blacksmith worked where the George car-park now is. It is possible that this was an extension of the original business.

The cottages fronting the Mead have been refurbished in recent years, and an extra cottage added on the southern end of the rank. Of the cottages facing Mead Lane, one is a part of the shop, and Redwood Cottage is separately occupied. Of the orchard and cider press nothing now remains, for it is no doubt built over.

Had it not been for the record of the series of deeds, we would know even less about 'Dibbins's'. Now that houses change hands frequently, and owners have Land Registry documents, ancient deeds are often destroyed as of no further use, but they are a priceless record of earlier owners. Blagdon Local History Society's archive contains photocopies of some deeds, and the Society will be pleased to accept deeds for preservation or for copying, as part of the ongoing work of searching for the history of the village.

Figure 4 – Redwood Stores as many older villagers remember it.
(Photograph, the late Les Barnes, copy in BLHS Archives)

References

Record of deeds lent to Somerset Record Office, DD/X/RW *(since retrieved by owner.)*
Schedule of deeds to Redwood Cottage *kindly supplied by Brian Redwood.*
Blagdon burial records, Somerset Record Office, *transcribed by Jenny Day, other transcripts by John Millar, and later transcripts from the parish register, coordinated by Rob Marley.*
Blagdon churchwardens' accounts, *transcribed by Olga Shotton.*
Blagdon census returns, *Somerset Record Office, transcribed by Olga Shotton and Rob Marley.*
Blagdon tithe map, *copied by Rob Marley from the parish copy.*
Blagdon apportionment index, *transcribed by Olga Shotton from the parish copy.*
Don Cole, *personal communication.*
Brian Redwood, *personal communication.*

Hannah More and her connections with Blagdon Part 1 — Early life, relationship with Langhorne, and the Mendip Schools

Elizabeth M. Harvey

Note on sources: words in italics are from primary sources, the most important of which is the journal of Hannah More's sister, Martha, from 1789 until 1799. In 1859 it was edited by Arthur Roberts and published as *Mendip annals.* The original is missing, but the printed version reads as if it was written at the time and Roberts' editing is quite distinct. Other primary sources are More's letters, especially her correspondence with William Wilberforce. The two early biographies of Hannah More, by Henry Thompson and William Roberts, were written soon after she died. Thompson only knew More after she left Barley Wood in Wrington and retired to Clifton in 1828, but he became Curate of Wrington only six months after she left and became acquainted with many people who had known her well in Wrington, Bath, Bristol and Clifton. His sources were private letters and living memories, but he omitted much as he was a High Church man and did not like her Evangelicalism. Roberts' biography was criticised by friends of Hannah More as he muddled the chronology and removed many colloquialisms from her letters, portraying her as a humourless, sanctimonious woman. Anne Stott, More's most recent biographer, has had the benefit of access to her largely unpublished letters.

Hannah More (1745-1833), author and philanthropist, was perhaps the most well known and influential woman in the England of her day. Her early life was spent as a schoolteacher in Bristol but, after regular visits to London, she became famous as a playwright and poet. Despite entering Horace Walpole's circle in 1780, Hannah became discontented with London society and, under the influence of John Newton, the Rector of St. Mary's, Coleman Street in London, she became involved in the Evangelical movement, writing conduct books – attempting to reform the morals of the aristocracy and middle classes – and cheap tracts to reform the morals of the poor. Her greatest achievement, however, was the creation of the Mendip schools, the most notorious of which was in Blagdon.

This essay, the first of two, concentrates on More's early life; her relationship with John Langhorne, Rector of Blagdon; the Evangelical movement within the Anglican church; her friendship with William Wilberforce, which led to the Mendip schools; the Sunday school movement; Hannah More's methods, teachers and aims; the attitude of the Mendip farmers; the opening of the Blagdon school in 1795 and its early success. The second essay will cover the "Blagdon Controversy," named after pamphlets published in 1801 by the then Curate of Blagdon, Thomas Bere, and detailing the dispute between himself and Hannah More over the behaviour of her Blagdon schoolteacher, Henry Young. The controversy led to the closure of the Blagdon school, and to vicious attacks on More in national journals, and became a *cause celebre* in the early 19th century.

Early life

Hannah More was born in 1745, the fourth daughter of Jacob More, master of a charity school in Fishponds, then a hamlet in the parish of Stapleton near Bristol. The five girls – Mary, Elizabeth, Sarah (Sally), Hannah and Martha (Patty) – were all born in the school house, which still stands in Manor Road. At a time when girls were not generally educated, they were first taught to read by their mother and then taught by their father. Hannah soon progressed beyond the boys at the school, and was given extra lessons in Latin and maths, whilst learning French from her eldest sister, Mary, who attended a French school in Bristol three times a week.

The schoolhouse at Fishponds
From a drawing by Henry Thompson, printed in his Life of Hannah More, 1838

Jacob's aim was to qualify his daughters "for the management of a ladies' school upon principles more befitting the requirements of responsible and reasonable beings" than existing girls' schools, where "intellectual pursuits were denounced as incapacitating women for domestic duties."[1]

In 1757 the girls moved to 6 Trinity Street near Bristol Cathedral, where Mary opened a school for young ladies, under the patronage of friends, when she was only twenty. Betty became the housekeeper while the younger three girls started as pupils. They were fortunate to be in Bristol at a time of increasing demand for female education amongst the wealthy merchants and tradespeople, who began to send their daughters to the new school with daughters of the gentry. The rise of the novel created a new reading public and an increasing interest in literature and drama. The Theatre Royal, which opened in King Street in 1766, was patronised by the sisters, who on occasions marched the whole school to a suitable play. The sisters read widely, attended public lectures and helped entertain distinguished visitors to the city, while their school became one of the most successful in the country.

In 1767 the school moved to a newly built house in Park Street[2], where they taught French, reading, writing, arithmetic, music and dancing to day girls and boarders, some of whom were daughters of the most influential men in Bristol. Hannah became a teacher in the school, where she wrote rhymes, stories and dramas for the children to act. She now read three languages and attended lectures in Bath on learned subjects including religion, philosophy and science.

Friendship with Dr Langhorne, Rector of Blagdon from 1766 to 1779

At about this time Hannah became engaged to William Turner, a local landowner who was twenty years her senior and who lived at Belmont House, Wraxall. The house still stands in the south east corner of what is now the Tyntesfield estate, belonging to the National Trust, on Belmont Hill. Mr Turner had two young cousins at the Park Street school who often visited him in the holidays, when they were allowed to bring two friends. Hannah and Martha More, being the two youngest teachers, were often invited. Hannah was then 22 and Turner, who valued her companionship and her opinion on the plans for his garden, proposed marriage although he was 20 years her senior. During their six year engagement he postponed the wedding three times and finally ended the engagement in 1773.[3]

In the late summer of that year Hannah was "recovering from an attack of ague at Uphill on the Somersetshire coast"[4] and probably feeling depressed after the end of her engagement. The village of Uphill "consisting of a few cottages occupied by fishermen and labourers, is situated at the conflux of the river Ax with the Bristol Channel. ... The huge promontory of Brean-down lying over against the village, and stretching its high ridge far into the sea. At ebb tide the beach is left dry from this down to Anchor Head, nearly half a mile below high water mark, and between the villages of Weston and Uphill is flat, composed of fine sand. ... This beach is almost covered with various kinds of shells. ... On the rocks are nerites, limpets and periwinkles, and there are several sorts of plants growing on the shore."[5]

While Hannah was convalescing at Uphill, the rector of Blagdon, John Langhorne, was convalescing at Weston. Langhorne's first wife, Ann,[6] had died giving birth to a son in 1768, when she was 32, and he had married his second wife, Isabella. Langhorne was a translator of Plutarch as well as being a poet, like Hannah. Weston then consisted of one irregular street half a mile in length, running through a woody vale beside a brook.[7] Hannah and Langhorne rode together on the sands, "Miss More, as the custom then was, on the pillion[8] behind her servant; and when it happened that either chanced to miss the other, a paper was placed in a cleft post near the water, generally containing some quaint remark, or a few verses."[9] On one occasion Langhorne wrote an improvised verse with his cane in the sand:

> *"Along the shore walked Hannah More;*
> *Waves! Let this record last;*
> *Sooner shall ye,*
> *Proud earth and sea,*
> *Than what she writes, be past"*[10]

Hannah replied with her riding whip:

> *"Some firmer basis, polished Langhorne choose,*
> *To write the dictates of your charming muse;*
> *Thy strains in solid characters rehearse,*
> *And be thy tablet lasting as thy verse."*[11]

"After this, the Misses More, Hannah especially, were frequent guests at Blagdon Parsonage."[12] One Sunday morning in May, Hannah and Sally left Bristol for Blagdon.

> *"... They quitted the town and the smoke that it yields,*
> *For the verdure and freshness of woods and of fields.*
> *Indulgent Apollo had sent them a day,*
> *The sweetest of summer, the mildest of May:*
> *...At length they arrive at the sign of the Bell,*
> *Which historians agree is the Blagdon Hotel;*
> *How brown was the toast! And how good was the tea!*
> *(Though of yellowish brown, somewhat ting'd with bohea.)*[13]
> *Now the village bell toll'd as a signal to pray,*
> *And, the breakfast unfinished, they hastened away:"*[14]

The Bell Inn, where Hannah and Sally had breakfast before hearing Langhorne preach at St Andrew's, was in Bell Square. After church they had dinner at the parsonage where they *'relished the wine and applauded the mutton.'*[15] The parsonage, which Hannah mistakenly calls the Vicarage, was then Blagdon House in Butcombe Road, now Station Road, and the village was "on the skirts of a beautiful rich valley, through which a small stream" ran, "fed by a variety of springs."[16] Langhorne, who enjoyed the company of intellectual women, began a lively, humorous correspondence with Hannah.

Meanwhile, in the winter of 1773-4, Hannah had made her first trip to London, with Sally and Patty, and was soon established in London society. For the next twenty years she made annual trips to the capital, making friends with Samuel Johnson, David Garrick, Joshua Reynolds, Sheridan and Elizabeth Montague. She became the acknowledged poet of the "Blue Stockings" and began to write for the theatre.

In February 1775 Langhorne wrote to Hannah complaining that she had *'slipped away to London'* without first visiting the Langhornes, as she had promised, and ending the letter with the following requests:

You are so obliging as to ask me for commands. ... Pray be so good as to go to the warehouse in George's Yard, Oxford Street, over against Dean Street, Soho, and buy me a bushel of Surinam potatoes for planting; which, with the paper instructions you will receive along with them, please send by the Bristol wagon, to the Queen's Head, Redcliffe Street.

Commands from my lady wife, who is neither poet nor philosopher, for you or for your good sister, viz. A crimson hat and cloak trimmed with blond lace.[17] *You are moreover desired to order the necessary materials, without leaving a plenipotentiary commission with the milliner. Neither is it to be violently modish.*[18]

Did Isabella Langhorne perhaps wear her not-too-violently-modish red hat and cloak to St. Andrew's on Sunday mornings? Sadly, in February 1776 she too died in childbirth. She was only 26.

In December John, in apparently good spirits, wrote Hannah a humorous account of his recent illness, as if it were a battle in the recent American War of Independence: *'General Bile was appointed commander-in-chief, and led the whole forces of Rheumatism Bay, Scurvy Island and Nervous Province, into the very centre and heart of my dominions, and drew up his army in form of battle.'*[19] He ended the letter with a description of his winter days in Blagdon:

At eight I rise, and that is almost as soon as the sun at this season makes himself known to us here. On my table I find a cup of cold chamomile tea with an infusion of orange peel; — dress, and come downstairs at nine, when I meet my breakfast, consisting of a basin of lean broth with a dry brown loaf, manufactured from corn of my own growing. Breakfast table cleared, I call for pen, ink, and paper, and recollect, not which of my correspondents I have longest been indebted to, but which humour leads me to write to. After this is performed, I apply a little to the laws of my country, to make myself a more useful citizen, and a better magistrate.
About twelve, if the day turns out fine, I order my horses, for exercise on Mendip, which at this time of year I can seldom effect; I am consequently obliged to seek exercise in measuring the length of my own hall. At two I dine, always upon one dish, and, by way of dessert, eat three or four golden pippins, the produce of my own orchard, and drink as many glasses of wine. But

then the afternoon — the solitary afternoon — Oh! For that the trash of the month comes in, and whether it makes me laugh or sleep, 'tis equally useful. The evening is divided between better books; music, and mending the fire, a roasted potato, a pint basin of punch, and to bed.

You have here the whole etiquette of my retirement, which in the summer is diversified by rural occupations and more agreeable amusements. In winter I am a better scholar, but in summer I am a better citizen. In the former season I attend only (as I do in this letter) to myself; in the latter I cultivate the ground, raise crops of corn, and hay, and flocks of sheep, and am useful to society.[20]

John Langhorne showed his admiration for Hannah's literary work by writing the prologue to her first play and a review of her poetry in the *Monthly review* for February 1776. He is believed to have proposed to her, but she did not accept.[21] In the words of Hannah's first biographer, "A habit of intemperance, in which he had vainly sought relief, under the pressure of domestic calamity, raised a barrier between him and persons of strict behaviour."[22] John Langhorne died an unhappy man in 1779, probably from alcohol poisoning. Hannah kept his entertaining letters, and the poems dedicated to her, until her own death. Here is one verse from *Stanzas written in the author's garden, On the promise of a visit from a lady.*

Blow, blow my sweetest rose!
For Hannah More will soon be here,
And all that crowns the ripening year
Should triumph where she goes [23]

Hannah More in 1780
Print after a painting by Frances Reynolds
by courtesy of Bristol Museum and Art Gallery

The Evangelical movement

Despite the puritanism of their paternal grandparents, the More sisters were brought up as Anglicans and regularly attended their parish church. They were also tolerant of Nonconformity, having many friends who were dissenters, and one of the first Evangelical preachers in Bristol, Dr James Stonhouse, was a neighbour in Park Street. In 1781 Hannah, discontented with London society, came under the influence of John Newton, an Evangelical Anglican clergyman, whose *'vital, experimental religion'*[24] changed the course of her life.

The Evangelical revival in 18th century England began with Whitefield and Wesley, the founders of Methodism, who, Hannah believed, *'first raised the tone of religion in the Church of England.'*[25] The next generation of Evangelicals were clergy and laypeople within the Anglican church, led by a group which later became known as the Clapham Sect. This remarkable group, who applied religion to everyday life, were "public-spirited, influential, highly respected, well-to-do business and professional men, their wives and families, living comfortable lives in comfortable homes, under the pastoral care of their spiritual guide, the wise and good father of the society, John Venn, Vicar of Clapham."[26] Their theology was based on atonement: men and women are, by nature, sinners and are redeemed by Christ's crucifixion, but need to demonstrate their salvation through godly living and charity, as the church had a duty to be involved in the secular world.[27] The Anglican Evangelicals believed that the church of Christ included all denominations, so the More sisters happily attended the dissenting chapel of the independent preacher William Jay, in Bath.

From 1780 to 1830 Evangelicalism influenced the upper and middle classes as much as Methodism did the lower classes. Evangelicals were dissuaded from leaving the Anglican church and wealthy Evangelical laymen, such as the banker MP, Henry Thornton, bought advowsons[28] for "serious"[50] clergy in strategically important churches.

Many 18th century philanthropists were Quakers, dissenters and Methodists but most belonged to the Evangelical party within the Anglican church. In 1786 Hannah became interested in the anti-slavery movement, begun by the Quakers, through an Evangelical friend, Lady Middleton. In the summer of 1787 Hannah met William Wilberforce who, having recently become an Evangelical, had been advised by Newton to use his parliamentary career in the service of God. In March he had found his greatest cause, on being invited to lead the parliamentary campaign against the slave trade, and in 1789 he helped Hannah find hers.

Cowslip Green and the first Mendip Sunday school

COWSLIP GREEN.

Cottage at Cowslip Green
From a drawing by Henry Thompson, printed in his 'Life of Hannah More', 1838

After ending their engagement William Turner had settled an annuity of £200 a year on Hannah, enabling her to be financially independent for the rest of her life. In 1785 she retired from teaching in Bristol and moved into a newly built thatched cottage at Cowslip Green. "It is only one storey high; the roof is thatch; a smooth lawn, with a few shrubs and trees, fronts the window of the drawing room, which looks towards the south. A border of flowers runs nearly round the walls. ... On one side of the lawn rises the abrupt hill on which the noble mansion of Aldwick Court has since been erected. To the south spreads the rich and sylvan valley, bounded by the dark outline of the Mendips, with their warm-tinted herbage and the dusky woods, casting out in bold relief the picturesque village of Blagdon, and the 'magic garden' of Mendip Lodge ... while between them the cottage roofs and venerable tower of Burrington."[29] Mendip Lodge was the home of Thomas Sedgwick Whalley, who will become important in the second part of this essay.

As the cottage was damp in winter Hannah spent the winters with her sisters in Park Street. They retired in 1789 "with great credit and in affluent circumstances,"[30] sold the school and, in 1790, bought a newly built house, 76 Pulteney Street, Bath, which became Hannah's new winter home. Patty, and sometimes the other sisters, spent the summers with her at Cowslip Green, where they were visited in August 1789 by William Wilberforce and his sister.

The More sisters suggested that their guests should visit the cliffs at Cheddar and the Wilberforces set off with a picnic lunch. On their return they told Hannah and Patty that the cliffs were very fine, but the poverty and distress of the people was dreadful and that *'something must be done for Cheddar'*. The four of them discussed many possible schemes and *'at length those schemes were adopted which led to the foundation of the different schools'*. [31]

In September 1789, when the sisters set off to enquire about the possibility of starting a Sunday school in Cheddar, Patty began to keep a journal. They soon discovered that the vicar of Cheddar lived in Oxford, the curate in Wells, there was one church service a week and *'as much knowledge of Christ in the interior of Africa'*.[32] They met opposition from a rich farmer, the chief despot of Cheddar, who believed that *'religion would be the ruin of agriculture; that it was a very dangerous thing, and had produced much mischief ever since it was introduced by the monks down at Glastonbury'*.[33] Hannah wrote to Wilberforce: *'We had a little plan which we hoped would secure their orchards from being robbed, their rabbits from being shot, their game from being stolen, and which might lower the poor rates. … They were as ignorant as the beasts that perish, intoxicated every day before dinner, and plunged in such vices as make me begin to think London a virtuous place'*.[34] Another farmer and his wife *'were utterly astonished at strangers coming there to do good … but were not insensible to the possible use of a Sunday-School, for they had heard of them, and read about them in the Bristol papers; and indeed their apples would be safer if the children were confined'*.[35] The sisters managed to find a suitable house and a suitable mistress, Mrs Barber, and the first Mendip Sunday school opened on 25th October 1789.[36]

The Sunday school movement

In the 1770s and 80s there was growing support for Sunday schools due to concern amongst churchmen and philanthropists over the perceived moral depravity of the lower classes. Wilberforce had not suggested such a school to Hannah but she did know of Raikes' Sunday schools in Gloucestershire,[37] there were Sunday schools in Churchill and Wrington and 55 charity schools, mostly endowed by private benefactors, existed in Somerset, although none were on the Mendips.[38] In 1788 Hannah visited Sarah Trimmer's school at Brentford, London,[39] which had received wide publicity, and found there "a scene of instruction and delight."[40]

Over the next six years Hannah and Patty opened schools at Shipham, Rowberrow, Sandford, Banwell, Congresbury, Yatton, Nailsea, Axbridge and Blagdon, attended by 1,000 children, with funds provided by Wilberforce and Thornton. By 1800 most of the smaller ones had been forced to close but the remaining "great schools" (Cheddar, Shipham, Nailsea and Blagdon) had adult schools as well as Sunday schools for children. Cheddar and Shipham had Women's Benefit Clubs and Blagdon had a small School of Industry.[41]

"The Mendip Scheme" (devised by the sisters for use in their schools)

1. The methods used

Hannah described her "method" in a letter to Mr Bowdler, a High Church man worried about subversion: '*My plan for instructing the poor is very limited and strict. They learn of week-days such coarse work as may fit them for servants. I allow no writing. My object has not been to teach dogmas and opinions, but to form the lower class to habits of industry and virtue. I know no way of teaching morals but by infusing principles of Christianity, nor of teaching Christianity without a thorough knowledge of Scripture. In teaching in our Sunday-schools, the only books we use are two little tracts called "Questions for the Mendip Schools",*[42]... *the Church Catechism (these are hung up in frames, half a dozen in a room), the Catechism broke into short questions, Spelling-books, Psalters, Common Prayer-book, and Bible. The little ones learn "Watts' Hymns for Children" – they repeat the collect every Sunday'.*[43]

She wrote to Wilberforce saying that the children started when they were six and were divided into two groups. '*In the morning, I open with one of the Sunday-School Prayers, from the "Cheap Repository Tracts".*[44] *I have a Bible class – Testament class – Psalter class. Those who cannot read at all are questioned out of the first little question book for the Mendip Schools'.* In the bible and testament class she always began with the parables, explaining them in a familiar manner, and she spent a long time on the first three chapters of Genesis, '*to establish them in the doctrine of the fall of man'*, which was central to Evangelical theology. The children read the same parts frequently so that they remembered the most important texts. '*I also encourage them by little bribes of a penny a chapter to get by heart certain fundamental parts of Scripture ... It is my grand endeavour to make everything as entertaining as I can, and to try to engage their affections; to excite them in the love of God, and particularly to awake their gratitude to their Redeemer.*'

When the children were tired, they revived their attention '*by standing up, and singing a hymn ... I never tried the system of terror, because I have found that kindness produces a better end by better means.*'

About five o'clock we dismiss the little ones with a prayer and a hymn. It would be an excellent method (and has been practised with success,) to invite the grown-up children and their parents, to come to school at six o'clock, and get some kind lady (which answers better than a teacher,) to read a little sermon to them — "Burden's Village Sermons" are very proper.

Those who attend four Sundays, without intermission, and come in time for morning prayer, receive a penny every fourth Sunday; but if they fail once, the other three Sundays go for nothing, and they must begin again. Once in every six or eight weeks I give a little gingerbread. Once a year I distribute little books according to merit – those who deserve most, get a Bible – second rate merit gets a prayer-book – the rest, Cheap Repository Tracts.

Once a year, each scholar receives some one article of dress, the boys, a hat, shirt, or pair of shoes, according to their wants – the big girls, a calico apron and cap – the little ones, a cap and a tippet of calico.[45]

2. The teachers

Hannah and Patty More were both gifted teachers who enjoyed their time with the children. They always used '*most homely language, full of anecdotes of the people round them, as well as the good people who lived in olden times*' and their lessons were '*full of practical piety – brought down into such minute detail as one never hears now*'.[46] They both worked very hard, visiting three parishes every Sunday, covering a circuit of ten to thirty miles on horseback, being out about thirteen hours and often spending the night in one of the villages.[47]

The sisters expected their teachers to make lessons '*pleasant by cheerful manners, by striking out a hymn when labour has been long continued, and by avoiding corporal punishment. Whatever makes them hate Sunday is wrong*'.[48] They first showed them by example, as on the long day spent at Shipham with Mr and Mrs Meyrick, '*putting them into our plans* which they received *with great humility and teachableness*'.[49]

They preferred to have a male and a female teacher, if possible from the lower middle class and with some experience, but more important were the qualities needed to make good Christians. The first Shipham mistress, Patience Seward, was a former farm servant who '*could read and write very prettily, was deeply serious,*[50] *and seemed pretty well acquainted with the scriptures*'.[51]

It was hard to find good male teachers, especially "spiritual teachers," and Hannah was wary of appointing teachers who showed signs of the "enthusiasm"[52] associated with Methodism. However she preferred this to formal religion and Wilberforce had advised her to use Methodists when she could not find Evangelicals.[56] Where it was difficult to find a good teacher, then a bad teacher was better than none, and in any case the sisters had little control over their teachers in the winter when they lived in Bath.

Aims of the Mendip scheme

1. Conversion to "true" Christianity

In her thesis on Hannah More, Anne Stott concluded: "It was the belief that they were dealing with the eternal destiny of the Mendip people ... that ultimately inspired Hannah and Patty More to undertake their work" and that Hannah's "over-riding aim was to convert the Mendip inhabitants, especially the children, to Evangelical religion."[54]

The parliamentary return of 1815 showed that 4,809 parishes in England and Wales had non-resident clergy. In many cases this was unavoidable as there was no parsonage. Cheddar had been without a resident clergyman for 40 years and in 1785, when the school opened, the church congregation numbered only twenty.[55] By 1801 it numbered seven hundred and extra pews had been installed.[56] Even where the clergy were resident, they were not inspected, as there had been no council for the management of internal affairs in the Church of England since 1717.[57] Consequently the clergy were generally remiss in their duty but, as women, Hannah and Patty could go into homes of "ignorant and depraved people where no clergyman would have been accepted." The sisters also had funds which were unavailable to Anglican clergy.[58]

Hannah used her influence to place Evangelical clergy in Shipham, Cheddar and Axbridge, where they would support the schools and be useful.

2. Creating obedient servants

Hannah's secondary aim was to "create an orderly population at a time of perceived moral crisis."[59]

Beilby Porteus, Bishop of Chester and a friend of Hannah, writing of '*the extreme depravity and licentiousness*' in Lancashire manufacturing towns, suggested that a '*very small degree of learning*' would not disqualify the poor '*from the most laborious employments in town or country*'. They should not be taught to write, merely '*to read … their Prayer Books, their Bible, and a few pious tracts … which enjoin under pain of eternal punishments and with the promise of eternal rewards, the great duties of sobriety, industry, veracity, honesty, humility, patience, content, resignation to the will of God and submission to the authority of their superiors*'.[60]

Not everyone agreed with Porteus, and there was a genuine fear that education would make the poor dissatisfied with their lot and lead to rebellion. This was, after all, the time of the French Revolution when, in England, "the friends of insurrection, infidelity and vice, carried their exertions so far as to load asses with their pernicious pamphlets, and to get them dropped, not only in cottages, and in the highways, but into mines and coal pits."[61] Thomas Paine's *Rights of Man,* written in a plain style for common readers and published in 1791-2, became a best seller. It claimed that the British constitution was founded on inherited privilege, called for the abolition of monarchy and aristocracy and advocated an egalitarian republic. Working men were soon joining reforming societies, calling for manhood suffrage and causing alarm amongst loyalists. How could the working class be kept in subordination?

One idea was through ballad sheets with loyalist ballads set to popular tunes. Another was cheap loyalist pamphlets and Hannah, with her knowledge of the poor, was perhaps the best person to write one. *Village politics*, the first of her *Cheap Repository Tracts*,[44] was written in 1792 at the suggestion of Hannah's friends. This fictitious dialogue between Tom Hod, the mason and Jack Anvil, the blacksmith, was set in a Somerset village and claimed to be written by a country carpenter, Will Chip. Tom, having picked up *The Rights of Man*, favours liberty and equality, while Jack represents Hannah's political views: equality is an illusion, as some are naturally stronger and more clever than others; a hierarchical society has a providential order in which the ruling classes exist to govern and use their wealth for benevolence and philanthropy, the merchants and farmers provide employment for the masses and the poor provide the labour force for the factories, mines, farms and homes of the more wealthy; it is best for the poor to be content with the station in life which God has allotted them. These views were shared by Edmund Burke, the philosophical statesman, and *Village politics* has been described as "Burke for beginners."[62]   (Burke had been MP for Bristol in Hannah's youth and frequently visited the Park Street house.)

"As a private individual" Hannah " was generous and compassionate to the poor around her. ... As a political writer, however, she refused to allow them any political rights beyond those enshrined in her idealised version of English law."[63]

3. Improvement in social welfare and industrial and domestic training for the children

The sisters' benefit clubs for poor women in Cheddar and Shipham provided relief for the sick and lying-in where there were no gentry to assist them. Any young woman "who continued to attend the school 'til her marriage, received on that occasion a pair of white stockings of Mrs More's own knitting, five shillings, and a Bible."[64] The women enjoyed an annual Feast Day when, after a church service, they had tea and cakes in the schoolroom.[65] The children in Cheddar and Shipham also had a feast day and a larger feast was held on top of Mendip for all the parishes, promoting solidarity between neighbourhoods and classes. "A separate table was spread for the children of each parish, where they were regaled with roast beef, plum pudding and cider." [66]

Their schools of industry taught the older girls and women sewing, spinning wool and knitting it into stockings which could be sold.[67] These girls were destined for domestic service, while the boys were destined to become agricultural labourers.

By providing clothing for the children, Hannah sometimes shamed the local farmers into making donations themselves.

The attitude of the Mendip farmers towards the education of their labourers

Although Hannah believed that the poor should be content with their station in life, she did not believe that they should be kept in ignorance. Not so the farmers, one of whom told Hannah and Patty that *'it was pre-ordained that they should be ignorant, and it was a shame to alter the decrees of God'*.[68] However, the farmers did not object to their own children being educated and Hannah was happy to teach reading and writing to these children at the weekday schools for an occasional small payment. (She did not teach writing in the Sunday schools.) But the farmers did not want their labourers to become more educated than themselves. The only way the farmers could maintain superiority was by acquiring superior knowledge at school in the evening, and this was how Hannah "increased their intelligence and respectability."[69]

As there were few gentry on the Mendips, the farmers were the village elite and had great influence locally as churchwardens, who "took a solemn oath to exercise a trust which they did not understand and occasionally resolved to betray."[70] The Overseers of the Poor were also farmers and "on them the comforts always, and the lives not infrequently, of the destitute absolutely depended."[71] Hannah's answer was to "teach compassion to those proud, ignorant and depraved"[72] farmers and eventually they were persuaded that education would make the poor hard working, self supporting and law abiding, thus reducing the work load of the local magistrates and the financial burden on the parish. The churchwardens and overseers of the poor were elected annually by the better-off householders, mostly farmers, and ruled the parish through the monthly vestry meeting, named after the church vestry where they met. In Blagdon they met once a month between 3pm and 5pm on Sunday, immediately after divine service.[73] The money needed to care for the parish poor was collected from these same householders and was known as the poor rate. The farmers in Cheddar had agreed to a school in their village because *'it might lower the poor rate'*, and eventually news of this school's success reached Blagdon.

The opening of the Blagdon Sunday school

Hannah later wrote of Blagdon, *'This place has helped to people the county gaol and Botany Bay beyond any I know of'*.[74] Thomas Bere, now a local magistrate and curate of this disreputable place, thought that by instructing the poor more, he would *'have occasion to commit them less'*,[75] so in the summer of 1795 he "waited on the sisters, to request they would open one of their schools in the parish. This they absolutely declined, declaring that neither their health (which had already greatly suffered by their exertions) nor their time, nor their finances would allow them to extend their personal superintendence beyond the range it had already taken."[76]

However, they were next visited by a deputation of the overseer and churchwarden, John Allen and Thomas Ozen,[77] with 'a humble petition that we would be so kind as to come and do their parish a little good'. Enquiring further, the sisters found that Blagdon 'exceeded in wickedness, if possible, any we had hitherto taken in hand' and 'this sudden desire of a Sunday-school partly arose from an awful scene having taken place just before in their parish, — a woman condemned to death for attempting to begin a riot, and purloining some butter from a man who offered it for sale at a price they thought unreasonable. This affecting event threw the village into the greatest consternation and terror'. One of the deputies, 'full six feet high, implored us with particular eagerness to come, because, he said, there were places where they were personally afraid to go. There is a little hamlet, called Charter House, on the top of Mendip, so wicked and lawless, that they report thieving to have passed down from father to son for the last forty years. The poor woman under sentence of death was an inhabitant of this place; and here it was that these tender-hearted churchwardens wished to send two nervous women'.[78]

'The extraordinary earnestness' of Mr Bere and the petitioners persuaded the sisters, and in October 1795 they opened 'one of the largest, most affecting, and interesting schools … composed of one hundred and seventy young people, the greater part from eleven to twenty years of age. … Nothing we had before experienced surpassed the ignorance of these poor creatures. … We opened … with some select psalms, a strong exhortation, and a suitable prayer. Very many tears were shed by the gentry who attended. In the afternoon we led them to church, where all country honours were duly paid. The men belonging to a large club attended with their ornamental sticks, and led the procession'.

Hannah wrote to Wilberforce: 'It was an affecting sight. Several of the grown-up youths had been tried at the assizes. Three were the children of a person lately condemned to be hanged; many, thieves; all ignorant, profane, and vicious beyond belief … and when the clergyman, a hard man, who is also the magistrate, saw these creatures kneeling round us, whom he had seldom seen but to commit or punish in some way, he burst into tears. … Some musical gentlemen, drawn from a distance by curiosity, (just as I was coming out of church with my ragged regiment, much depressed to think how little good I could do them), quite unexpectedly struck up the beautiful and animating anthem, "Inasmuch as ye have done it to one of the least of these ye have done it unto Me." It was well performed and had a striking effect'.[79]

Thomas Bere, the curate, was also the Rector of Butcombe and lived in Blagdon House, as Langhorne had before him. It is interesting, in the light of subsequent events, that he impressed Hannah as a "hard man" as early as 1795.

HOUSE AT BLAGDON, WHERE MRS. MORE OPENED HER SCHOOL.

The Blagdon Sunday school
From a drawing by Henry Thompson, printed in his 'Life of Hannah More', 1838

Room was found for the new school at a house in Church Street, now Hannah More House, and Mr and Mrs Younge,[80] teachers at the Nailsea school, where they had quarrelled with two farmers, were moved to Blagdon. The Younges, who came from Bath, had originally been recommended to Hannah for their *'religious zeal and industry'*,[81] but their Methodist sympathies and their quarrelsome nature did not cause her to hesitate when she needed teachers for Blagdon. In 1794 Patty had written in her journal, *'Pride, and a consciousness of really tolerable abilities, seem to be the besetting sins of Mr Younge'*.[82] Hannah later admitted to Wilberforce that Younge was a *'disciple of John Wesley's'*.[83]

The sisters did not visit the new school for several Sundays and, when they did, they found that numbers had risen and that many had made progress. *'The first question book was learned through by many, and the grown-up ones understood tolerably the first twenty chapters of Genesis.*[84] *The Blagdon farmers even came secretly at night to be taught themselves'*.[85] They spent the last Sunday at Blagdon before retiring to Bath for the winter and found the school *'improving in a surprising and extraordinary manner. They already sing, repeat a good deal, and understand a little ... and there is a farmer's daughter who promises well'*.[86] The attendance figures for Blagdon which Hannah sent to Wilberforce in 1795 were: Sunday school 185; weekly day school [probably farmers' children] 30; weekly night school [farmers] 30.[87]

During the winter the sisters received progress reports from the schools and a letter from Blagdon reported that '*twenty-seven, instead of the odd seven, were at the sacrament, Christmas-day, and the school very full. Most of these children shew good capacities, and are making very rapid progress indeed*'.[88]

In May 1796 Hannah and Patty returned to Cowslip Green and began their usual round of the schools. They now '*gave the first rewards at Blagdon, to a full, flourishing and well-informed school. The overseers … regularly visit the school … standing with great humility for hours at a time. They also come in the week, and submit to be taught with the simplicity of children. …We are extremely anxious, and Mrs Bere still more so, that our Sunday evening reading might be introduced at Blagdon; and it accordingly took place, to our no small joy, the Sunday following, with great success*'.[89]

The sisters had occasionally used young men from their Cheddar school to help at Blagdon as under teachers but, to their surprise, some of the young people at Blagdon '*were already becoming tolerable teachers*'.[90]

In September 1796 Hannah wrote to Newton: '*Of nearly two hundred children, many of them grown-up, hardly any had ever seen the inside of a church since they were christened. … Finding the heads of the parish (farmers) quite as ignorant as the labourers, we devised a method, at the outset, of saving their pride, by setting one evening a week on purpose for their instruction. Above twenty, including their wives, attend, and many seem to be brought under serious*[50] *impressions. One great benefit is … the removal of that great gulf which has divided the rich and poor in these country parishes; by making them meet together; whereas before they hardly thought they were children of one common father*'.[74]

In the winter the sisters returned to Bath and received two good letters from Blagdon in early 1797. '*The Sunday evening readings go on well. One of the Stephenses from Charter House (who had been tried for murder, as Mr Bere told us) was beginning to attend both the school and evening reading, with much attention and some apparent seriousness. … this young man's continued attendance may probably hereafter influence others at Charter House*'.[91] Another letter reported that '*two sessions and two assizes are passed, and a third approaching, and neither as prosecutor nor prisoner, plaintiff nor defendant, has any of this parish (once so notorious for crimes and litigation) appeared; and, moreover, warrants for woodstealing, pilfering, etc, are quite out of fashion*'.[92]

In December the sisters left for Bath, returning to Mendip in May 1798. Patty wrote in her journal: '*Blagdon we found in a steady, uniform course of apparent growth in grace; great decorum; great peaceableness. The school in a good state of improvement. The evening reading was very interesting and affecting. The whole people stood up, and, with the modesty and simplicity of children, suffered the master to stand forward and state to us the particulars of their behaviour during the winter. It was an extraordinary proceeding; for the parish officers were among the number. It was at the desire of the justice we were to be publicly informed of the extraordinary decorum of the men on the day of their club, which had just taken place, and their conduct, it seems, had struck all parties, as well as themselves. We ventured to infer from this that religion was evidently operating upon their conduct, and were much rejoiced at it'.*[93]

The '*great peaceableness*' of the school proved to be the calm before the storm. In the autumn of 1798 Thomas Bere heard that Henry Younge was holding '*private school meetings*' for adults on Monday evenings and sent Sarah, his wife, to the school to find out what was going on. What happened in Blagdon after this date, and the national publicity it received when Bere decided to publish a pamphlet about it in 1801, will be the subject of Part Two. The "Blagdon Controversy" took its name from Bere's pamphlet and divided local clergy, bishops and influential laity, for Hannah had friends in high places. Her name was vilified by journalists in the *Anti-Jacobin review* who failed to realise she shared the journal's loyalties to the crown. All her good work was misconstrued as the journal incorrectly equated Evangelicalism with political unrest, but the journal was correct in recognising that the dispute involved '*questions of more importance*' than were '*superficially apparent*'.[94]

References and notes

1   Henry Thompson, *The Life of Hannah More with Notices of her Sisters* (London, Cadwell, 1838), pp.6-7.

2   Then the first house in Park Street, now number 43.

3   Henry Thompson ... pp.15-20.

4   *Ibid*, p.22.

5   John Collinson, *The History and Antiquities of the County of Somerset* (1791), vol.III, p.608.

6   Ann was the daughter of Robert Cracroft of Hackthorn, Lincolnshire. Langhorne was tutor to her brothers.

7   John Collinson ... p.610.

8   A pillion was a cushion attached behind the saddle on a horse for a second rider, usually a woman.

9   Henry Thompson ... p.22.

10   *Ibid*.

11   *Ibid*.

12   *Ibid*.

13   Bohea is poor quality tea, being from the last crop of the season.

14   Henry Thompson ... pp.389-92: Appendix IV, poem written by Hannah More and entitled "The Expedition of a Female Poet and a Female Printer to Blagdon Vicarage." Thompson was not aware that it had ever been published.

15   Henry Thompson ... p.392.

16   John Collinson ... p.569.

17   "Blond lace" is made of silk.

18   William Roberts, *Memoirs of the Life and Correspondence of Mrs Hannah More* (London, R.B. Seeley and W. Burnside, 1838), 3rd ed., vol.I, pp.20-22.

19   William Roberts ... p.25.

20   *Ibid*, pp.27-28.

21   Henry Thompson ... p.21.

22   William Roberts ... p.18.

23   *Ibid*, p.28.

24   Letter from Hannah More to Mrs Boscawen, 1780, cited in William Roberts ... p.188.

25   More to Wilberforce, 10th August 1820, Wilberforce MSS, Bodleian Library Oxford, cited in Anne M. Stott, *Hannah More: evangelicalism, cultural reformation and loyalism* (unpublished PhD thesis, University College London, 1998.)

26   M.G. Jones, *Hannah More* (Cambridge University Press, 1952), p.93.

27   D.W. Bebbington, *Evangelicalism in modern Britain: a history from the 1730s to the 1980s* (London, Unwin Hyman, 1989)

28   The right of presentation to a church benefice.

29   Henry Thompson ... pp.69-70.

30   William Roberts ... vol.II, p.203.

31   Arthur Roberts (ed), *Mendip annals: or a narrative of the charitable labours of Hannah and Martha More in their neighbourhood, being the journal of Martha More* (London, 1859), p.13.

32   *Ibid*, p.16.

33   *Ibid*, p.14.

34   *Ibid*, p.18.

35   *Ibid*, p.15.

36   *Ibid*, p.23.

37   Raikes aimed to teach reading, catechism and morals to ragged children who roamed the streets and to take them to church on Sundays. His schools were imitated on a national scale.

38   P. Belham, *The origins of elementary education in Somerset, with particular reference to Hannah More in the Mendips* (MA thesis, University of Bristol, 1953), cited in A. M. Stott thesis.

39   Sarah Trimmer was a High Church woman. Her schools were funded by aristocratic ladies and she used existing teachers, working with the Vicar of Ealing, whose idea it was. Trimmer was a friend of Bishop Porteus, who was also a friend of More.

40   William Roberts ... vol.II, p.115.

41   Martha More to Lady Waldegrave, cited in A.M. Stott thesis.

42   Written by Hannah and Martha More.

43   *Mendip annals,* p.6.

44   Little books written by the More sisters and Evangelical friends.

45   "*Hints for schools*" in letter from More to Wilberforce, 1801, cited in William Roberts ... vol.III, pp.150–15.

46   Marianne Thornton, Thornton Papers, Cambridge University Library, cited in A.M. Stott thesis.

47   Henry Thompson ... p.100.

48   More to Wilberforce, Wilberforce Collection, Duke University (Durham, N. Carolina), cited in A.M. Stott thesis.

49   *Mendip annals*, p.219.

50   "Serious" meant Evangelical.

51   *Mendip annals*, p.29.

52   "Enthusiasm" was an 18th century term for fanaticism.

53   Wilberforce to More, cited in Robert, Isaac & Samuel Wilberforce, *The life of William Wilberforce,* vol.1, p.247.

54   Anne M. Stott thesis.

55   Henry Thompson ... p.87.

56   *Ibid*, p.94.

57   There had been no council to manage the affairs of the Church of
      England since the suspension of Convocation in 1717.

58   Henry Thompson ... p.110.

59   Anne M. Stott thesis.

60   Beilby Porteus, *A Letter to the Clergy in the Diocese of Chester concerning
      Sunday Schools* (London, 1786), cited in M.G. Jones, *Hannah More*
      (Cambridge, 1952), p.134.

61   William Roberts ... vol.II, p.422.

62   M.G. Jones ... p.134.

63   Kierman, *Evangelicalism and the French Revolution,* p.50.

64   Henry Thompson ... p.101.

65   *Ibid*, pp.102-3.

66   *Ibid*, pp.104-5.

67   More to Wilberforce, 1795, cited in William Roberts ... vol.II, pp.446-7.

68   *Mendip annals,* p.208.

69   Henry Thompson ... p.98.

70   *Ibid*, p.97.

71   *Ibid*, p.97.

72   *Ibid*, p.97.

73   Blagdon Vestry minutes for 1759.

74   More to Newton, 15th September 1796, cited in William Roberts ... vol.II,
      p.468.

75   More to Zachary Macauly, 6th January 1796, cited in William Roberts ...
      vol.II, p.460.

76   William Roberts ....vol II,

77   Blagdon churchwardens' accounts for 1795 name John Allen and Thomas
      Ozen as churchwardens and it is likely that they also acted as overseers of
      the poor.

78   *Mendip annals*, pp.166-7.

79   *Ibid*, pp.167-9.

80   Martha More spelled the name Younge, but it was sometimes spelled
      Young.

81   *Ibid*, p.55.

82   *Ibid*, p.128.

83   More to Wilberforce, 2nd September 1800, Wilberforce Collection, Duke
      University, cited in A.M. Stott thesis.

84   *Mendip annals,* p.170.

85   More to Wilberforce, 25th January 1796, Wilberforce Collection, Duke
      University, cited in A.M. Stott thesis.

86   *Mendip annals*, p.172.

87   Letters from More to Wilberforce in 1795, cited in A.M. Stott thesis.

88   *Mendip annals*, pp.174-5.

89   *Ibid*, p.195.

90   *Ibid*, p.183.

91   *Ibid*, p.196.

92   *Ibid*, p.198.

93   *Ibid*, p.204.

94   *Anti-Jacobin review and magazine*, July 1801.

Select bibliography

Printed primary source

More, Martha, *Mendip annals; or, The narrative of the charitable labours of Hannah and Martha More*, ed. Arthur Roberts (London, 1859.)

Secondary sources

William Roberts, *Memoirs of the life and correspondence of Hannah More*, 3rd ed. 4 vols. (London, 1838.)

Henry Thompson, *The Life of Hannah More with notices of her sisters* (London, 1838.)

Mary Alden Hopkins, *Hannah More and her circle* (New York: Longmans, Green, 1947.)

M.G. Jones, *Hannah More* (Cambridge: Cambridge University Press, 1952.)

P. Belham, *The Origins of elementary education in Somerset, with particular reference to the work of Hannah More in the Mendips* (MA thesis, University of Bristol, 1953.)

Jeremy and Margaret Collingwood, *Hannah More, the woman who brought hope to England's darkest places* (Oxford: Lion Publishing, 1990.)

Anne M. Stott, *Hannah More: evangelicalism, cultural reformation, and loyalism* (PhD thesis, University College London, 1998.)

Anne M. Stott, *Hannah More: the first Victorian* (Oxford University Press, 2003.)

THE RAILWAY IN BLAGDON

Mike Adams

Early optimism

The Wrington Vale Light Railway (WVLR) opened to public acclaim on 4th December 1901. School children in the area, including Blagdon, had a holiday, and some firms closed for the day and gave free tickets to their workpeople. About 1,500 people travelled on the first day, requiring extra coaches. The entry in Blagdon School log for 4th December is simply:

> 'Whole Holiday on the occasion of the opening of the Wrington Vale Light Railway.
> I record the fact that the directors gave the children a free ride to Burrington.'

This was after a local benefactor had offered to pay for them. They marched as a group from the school to the station, picking up sweets on the way from Mr Wood's shop near the school. They also had to walk back from Burrington after the one-way trip! In the early 1900s there were just over 140 children attending. This number increased to over 180 during the construction of the WVLR and Yeo Reservoir.

Figure 1 – an early advertising postcard (Olga Shotton)

After the initial enthusiasm and excitement, the passenger service was destined to last just 30 years. It may seem folly now that a branch line was built to end at Blagdon, a seemingly insignificant Somerset village. To understand why this happened, we need to cast our minds back to the planning stage near the end of the 19th century, when local transport was horse-drawn. The valley area around the proposed railway, including Blagdon, possessed some of the best pasture land in Somerset and produced a plentiful supply of dairy products which, being highly perishable, needed to be transported daily to market. Around 120,000 people were living within striking distance of the proposed railway and it was thought that there would be no shortage of regular fare-paying passengers. Bristolians could enjoy days out in the Mendips, notably at Burrington, with its famous Rock of Ages, and at Blagdon Lake, which duly opened to the public for fishing in 1904. The prospects for a railway seemed good.

*Figure 2 - Photo of Blagdon Station displayed in Blagdon Pumping Station
(John Gallop)*

Figure 3 – Blagdon Station c1904 (Veronica Counsell)
*At the top right is the name J. Nelson. He was the village postmaster; presumably he commissioned this
postcard to sell in Blagdon Post Office in the High Street. To the left of the Blagdon sign is the static carriage
which served as porters' accommodation and horse box. To the right is an iron gent's urinal and to its right on
the platform is an 18 gallon milk churn. Behind the Blagdon sign in the distance is Inspection House, which
was used by senior railway managers when visiting Blagdon. The shed on the far right was to store parcels.*

The planning stage

The original idea in 1881 was to connect Yatton on GWR's main Bristol & Exeter Railway, which had opened in 1841, with Farrington Gurney and the Somerset coalfield. Coal wagons could then by-pass Bristol on their way to the south west. This scheme failed to get sufficient support, but then the proposal for the WVLR was put forward, which would start at Congresbury and end at Blagdon via Wrington, Langford and Burrington. Congresbury was the first station after Yatton on the existing Cheddar Valley Railway (affectionately known as the Strawberry Line), which had opened in 1869.

Two major factors seem to have tipped the balance in favour of the WVLR scheme – the passing of the new Light Railways Act (LRA) in 1896 and the construction of the Yeo reservoir (now Blagdon Lake). The LRA enabled new branch lines to be set up by a Light Railway Order (LRO) instead of an Act of Parliament. It also allowed them to be constructed to a lower specification than main lines, making them much cheaper. See Appendices 1 and 2 for more details.

Bristol Waterworks Company (BWW) had begun the construction of its reservoir in 1891. In the permanent exhibition at Blagdon Waterworks there is a large photograph of Blagdon station in the very early 1900s with two lines of trucks (fig 2). In this photograph the static porters' carriage is not yet in place. The exhibition caption states the railway was 'built to serve the lake construction'. On the side of many of the trucks in the large photograph can be seen, 'John Wainwright & Company, Moon's Hill Stone, Cranmore, GWR.' Clearly the railway was not built solely to serve Bristol Waterworks in Blagdon; the date for completion of the reservoir is recorded as 1901, the year the railway took its first passengers. However, much building stone and aggregate was required in building the waterworks (and the railway itself). Also it was predicted that its steam–powered pumping engines would require a regular supply of coal, around 3,000 tons per year, which was best delivered by rail.

Plans come to fruition

Developments followed one another quickly. A consortium applied for the LRO in 1896 and a notice appeared in the *Bristol Times and Mirror* on 21st November 1896. The six-man consortium consisted of the MP for North Somerset, Colonel Evan Henry Llewellyn (Langford Court), Edward Stock Hill of the well-known ship-building family in Bristol (Hazel Manor, Compton Martin), Edward Bush (Alveston), Thomas Branfill Harrison (Wrington), Benjamin Edward Somers (Langford) and Henry Herbert Wills of the well-known tobacco family in Bristol (Barley Wood, Wrington).

The notice listed a number of landowners or occupiers in Blagdon who would be affected – Joseph Cryer, William Young, Mrs Annie Carpenter, Thomas Williams, Sir William Henry Wills, Richard Wilding, George Edwards, Joseph William Panes, William Lyons, Morley Gallop, Bristol Waterworks Company, Pethick Brothers,

William Cann and William Day (fig 4). See Appendix 3 for details of land and landowners from whom land was requisitioned.

The necessary public enquiry took place in 1897 at Wrington, the Board of Trade confirmed the Order in 1898, GWR agreed to build and operate the line in 1899 and it opened on Monday 4th December 1901. There were four trains each way daily, one of which was a mixed passenger and goods train. Occasional extra goods trains were run as required.

It is worth noting that Colonel Evan Llewellyn became a director of GWR in 1898 and was also a director of BWW. Sir William Henry Wills (later Lord Winterstoke), a director of the famous family tobacco company W.D. & H.O. Wills, lived in Blagdon at Coombe Lodge Estate, a short distance south of the railway. He arranged to have his own short siding which branched off by the Waterworks siding, 792 yards before Blagdon station. He used the railway primarily for his farm and other goods, which were hauled up Lays Lane to the estate. Occasionally he used the siding personally – when he visited his farm in Devizes he would often return on the last train.[1] The BWW branch again branched into two before entering their building to supply the two sets of steam pumping engines.

On 23rd November 1901 Blagdon Village Club was opened, of which Sir William was the benefactor. He is reported as saying on that occasion that, '*he thought that the opening of the railway would do a great deal for Blagdon, for they would be able to leave there at 8.00 in the morning and be in Bristol by 9.00, which he knew would suit his agricultural friends very well, especially on Thursdays – market day in Bristol. If their wives wanted to go to Bristol with their produce, they would be able to be there long before the ladies of Clifton got down in the city. He could not help thinking that Blagdon was not going to take a back seat. The land offered opportunities for building that would be very attractive to the people of Bristol. The fishing in the district was, he believed, some of the best in England ...*'

In practice WVLR trains from Blagdon continued on to Yatton after Congresbury to enable passengers to connect with the main line without having to change at Congresbury. Thus, according to the timetable published under the name of J.L. Wilkinson, General Manager GWR Paddington, in November 1901, the following journey to London became possible (fig 5):

WVLR – depart Blagdon 8.00am, arrive Yatton 8.30am; Main Line – depart Yatton 8.37am, arrive Bristol Temple Meads 9.06am, arrive London Paddington 12.53pm.

A day trip to London was impractical for many purposes, because the last return was: London 3.00pm, Bristol T.M. 6.10pm, Yatton 6.38pm/6.50pm, Blagdon 7.20pm.

However, passengers could spend from 9.06am to 6.10pm in Bristol, making it viable for work or leisure.

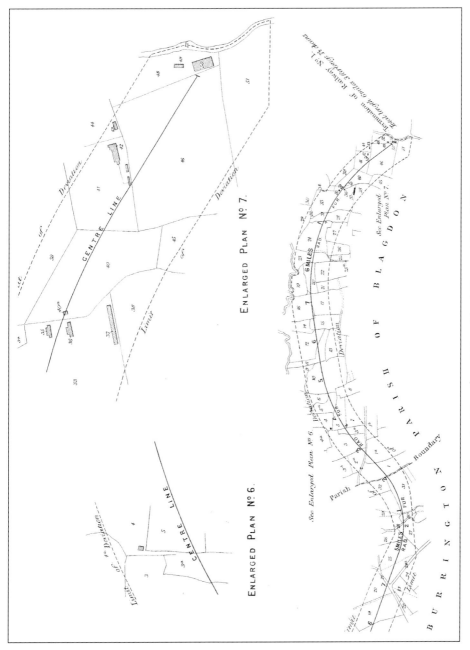

Figure 4 - Map of requisitioned land (Somerset Record Office)

GREAT WESTERN RAILWAY.

OPENING

OF THE

WRINGTON VALE

LIGHT RAILWAY.

On WEDNESDAY, DECEMBER 4th, 1901,

This Line will be opened for Public traffic with Stations at

WRINGTON, LANGFORD, BURRINGTON

AND

BLAGDON.

DOWN TRAINS.		WEEK DAYS ONLY.			
		A.M.	A.M.	A.M.	P.M.
London (Paddington)	dep.	...	7 25	11 45	3 0
Bristol (Temp. Meads)	,,	8 5	11 20	3 25	6 10
Yatton	arr.	8 33	11 40	3 45	6 38
Taunton	dep.	...	9 43	1 35	4 48
Weston super Mare	,,	7 45	10 54	3 25	6 0
Yatton	arr.	8 4	11 7	3 39	6 13
Clevedon	dep.	7 55	10 50	3 12	6 0
Yatton	arr.	8 3	10 58	3 20	6 8
		A.M.	A.M.	P.M.	P.M.
YATTON	dep.	8 40	11 50	3 50	6 50
Congresbury	arr.	8 45	11 54	3 53	6 53
Wells	dep.	7 20	9 50	2 15	4 55
Axbridge	,,	7 48	10 22	2 48	5 30
Congresbury	arr.	8 4	10 42	3 8	5 50
Congresbury	dep.	8 44	12 0	3 54	6 54
Wrington	,,	8 52	12 11 MIXED	4 2	7 2
Langford	,,	8 59	12 23	4 9	7 9
Burrington	,,	9 5	12 34	4 15	7 15
BLAGDON	arr.	9 10	12 40	4 20	7 20

UP TRAINS.		WEEK DAYS ONLY.			
		A.M.	A.M.	P.M.	P.M.
BLAGDON	dep.	8 0	9 35	2 35	5 20
Burrington	,,	8 4	9 39	2 39	5 24
Langford	,,	8 8	9 43	2 43	5 30
Wrington	,,	8 14	9 49	2 49	5 40
Congresbury	arr.	8 23	9 58	2 58	5 55
Congresbury	dep.		10 0	3 40	6 1
Axbridge	arr.		10 20	4 0	6 20
Wells	,,		10 50	4 30	6 50
Congresbury	dep.	8 24	9 59	2 59	6 0
YATTON	arr.	8 30	10 5	3 5	6 7
Yatton	dep.	8 58	10 25	3 37	6 33
Clevedon	arr.	9 6	10 33	3 45	6 40
Yatton	dep.	8 33	11 1	3 29	6 26
Weston super Mare	arr.	8 57	11 25	3 45	6 40
Taunton	,,	10 13	12 47	5 43	8 56
Yatton	dep.	8 37	10 19	3 30	6 13
Bristol (Temp. Meads)	arr.	9 6	10 50	4 0	6 35
London (Paddington)	,,	12 35	2 40	7 0	10 10

Passengers, Parcels and Goods traffic will be dealt with at Wrington, Langford and Blagdon, and Passengers only at Burrington.

PADDINGTON, November, 1901. **J. L. WILKINSON, General Manager.**

Wyman & Sons, Ltd., Printers, [illegible], Carter Lane, Doctors Commons, E.C. [illegible]

A poster time table for the opening of the Wrington Vale Light Railway, Wednesday 4th December, 1901. *Author's Collection*

Figure 5 – The first timetable 1901 (Colin Maggs)

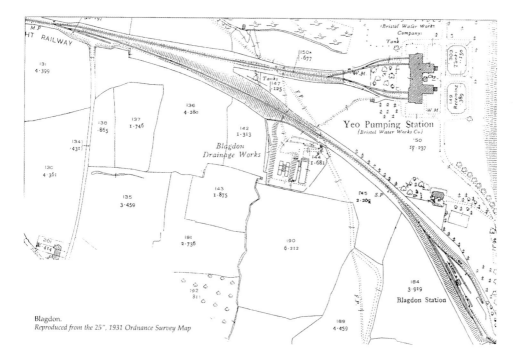

Figure 6 - Map of the completed station site (Colin Maggs)

The railway meets competition

Before the First World War a late train was run on Saturdays as an experiment, leaving Blagdon at 7.25pm and returning 8.30pm from Yatton. It was withdrawn in 1915 and never replaced – the hoped-for passengers were not forthcoming even then. This was one of the first of a series of economies which continued until eventual closure, as the railway struggled to adjust to the growth of bus services and private motor cars. Blagdon station was correctly positioned in the valley from the point of view of the whole railway, but it was very inconvenient for the village. Passengers had to climb half a mile up the steep Station Road[2], gaining 200 feet in height, to get to the village. Even goods destined for the Wills Estate began to be unloaded at Burrington rather than their private siding, to avoid the steep climb up Lays Lane. Charlie Simkin had a bungalow at the station entrance[3], from which he operated a horse and wagon transport service. His horse often slipped on the hill in bad weather conditions.

Although passenger numbers were disappointing, the goods traffic made the line pay – particularly coal and milk, which was transported in large 17-gallon churns. Economies continued apace. On 31st March 1924 the engine shed at Blagdon station was closed, the engine being stationed overnight at Yatton; the timetable was adjusted accordingly. Then station masters were replaced by senior porters at

Langford and Burrington on 29th December 1925 and at Blagdon on 6th January 1926. The whole branch was then controlled by the Wrington station master. Bristol Tramway Company introduced its autobus route from Blagdon to Bristol on 22nd December 1921, and from Bristol to Bridgwater, through Langford, on 26th March 1921. The writing was on the wall for the railway. During the 1926 General Strike, in which railway workers had a prominent role, Nestlé expanded its milk collections directly from farms by lorry.[4] The railway recovered only part of their previous milk traffic after the strike. Coal began to be supplied by road. Silvey's coal merchants brought their coal from Wales by ship into Bristol Docks and loaded it on to lorries which delivered directly to Blagdon pumping station.[5] The line was finally closed to passengers on 14th September 1931 and remained open only for the single daily goods train and 'specials'. It has been said that it was the last branch line to be opened in England and the first to close. Only three 'specials' are known:

In 1934 a party of pilgrims travelled to Burrington to visit the 'Rock of Ages' made famous by the hymn composed by the Reverend Toplady when he was curate of Blagdon in the early 1760s but published later in 1776. It is possible that similar trips were made but they are unknown.

On 8th September 1948 the complete stock and chattels of a farm were brought to Blagdon station from Maidenhead to be transported on to West Town Farm in Nempnett Thrubwell. The cows had to be milked on the platform. This event has gone down into local folklore and is often quoted.[6]

On 28th April 1957 the London Branch of the Railway Correspondence and Travel Society ran their North Somerset Rail Tour (fig 7). The route is thought to have been hauled by no. 30453 "King Arthur" from London Waterloo to Reading General; no. 3440 "City of Truro" from Reading General to Bristol Temple Meads; LMS Class 2, 2-6-2, tanks nos. 41202 and 41203 to visit Bristol area branches (Bristol harbour, WVLR and Burnham-on-Sea) and nos. 3440 and 5528 from Bristol to Radstock, Frome, Westbury and returning to London Paddington. They could only travel as far as Wrington on the WVLR as the rest of the railway had been closed since 1st November 1950. There were eight coaches.

Holiday or camp coach

The GWR was enterprising in trying many ways of gaining revenue by taking advantage of local amenities. It had a system of static coaches adapted for holidays (fig 9). A six-berth railway coach was parked on the siding behind Blagdon station in 1935 in the hope that it would attract business, particularly from anglers visiting Blagdon Lake but perhaps also holidaymakers simply wanting to explore the area. It probably lasted until the Second World War and it seems everything was supplied – cutlery, crockery, bed clothes down to dusters. Clean linen at the beginning of a stay was delivered from GWR's laundry in Swindon via Yatton and the WVLR guard's van. Fresh water also had to be delivered in the van from Congresbury.

Figure 7 - RCTS special stopped at Wrington 28th April 1957 (author's collection)

Figure 8 – Ticket showing route (author's collection)

CAMP COACHES

FOR

HAPPY HOLIDAYS

Railway coaches fully equipped with bedclothes, linen, cutlery, crockery, etc., and specially fitted to accommodate 6, 8 or 10 persons are available for hire at carefully selected beauty spots in Dorset, Somerset, Devon, Cornwall, Thames Valley, Wye Valley, Central and South Wales and the Cambrian Coast.

A list of these sites is shown below :

DORSET
Abbotsbury (Type " C ")
Bridport West Bay (Type " C ")
Portesham (Type " C ")
Powerstock (Type " C ")
Upwey (Type " B ")

SOMERSET
Axbridge (Type " B ")
Blagdon (Type " C ")
Blue Anchor (Type " C ")
Cheddar (Type " C ")
Congresbury (Type " C ")
Stogumber (Type " B ")
Winscombe (Type " A ")
Wookey (Type " A ")

DEVON
Ashton (Type " B ")
Avonwick (Type " A ")
Bampton (Type " C ")
Dawlish Warren (Type " D ")
East Anstey (Type " B ")
Gara Bridge (Type " C ")
Ide (Type " B ")
Loddiswell (Type " C ")
Lustleigh (Type " C ")

CORNWALL
Fowey (Type " C ")
Luxulyan (Type " A ")
Marazion (Type " C ")
Penryn (Type " C ")
Perranwell (Type " A ")
St. Agnes (Type " C ")

THAMES VALLEY
Wargrave (Type " B ")

WYE VALLEY
Kerne Bridge (Type " B ")
Tintern (Type " B ")

SOUTH WALES
Manorbier (Type " B ")

CENTRAL WALES
Dinas Mawddwy (Type " B ")
Dolgelley (Type " B ")
Erwood (Type " B ")
Llangollen (Type " B ")
Newbridge-on-Wye (Type " B ")
Rhayader (Type " B ")
Trawscoed (Type " B ")

CAMBRIAN COAST
Aberayron (Type " C ")
Abererch (Type " C ")
Afon Wen (Type " C ")
Barmouth Junction (Type " C ")
Borth (Type " C ")
Bow Street (Type " C ")
Dyffryn-on-Sea (Type " C ")
Fairbourne (Type " C ")
Llanilar (Type " B ")
Talsarnau (Type " C ")
Towyn (Type " C ")

The coaches are let at the following rates :—

Type of coach	No. of berths	Rent per week	Minimum number of rail tickets to be purchased
" A "	6	£3	4
" B "	6	£3	4
" C "	8	£4	6
" D "	10	£5	8

Write at once for full particulars to : **SUPERINTENDENT OF THE LINE, Great Western Railway, Paddington Station, London, W.2.**

Figure 9 – Advertisement for holiday coaches
(Veronica Counsell)

Brief revival

There was a brief revival of WVLR during the Second World War. It was needed to transport sacks for processing at Downey's sack factory on the Blagdon station site.[7] In addition, a variety of war materials was brought to storage depots in the Wrington and Burrington area. Blagdon, Burrington and Langford stations were closed finally on 1st November 1950, the latter two being demolished in 1958. For some reason the Blagdon station was left untouched, except by vandals, until it was bought by David and Veronica Counsell for conversion to a private dwelling, now called Little Halt. Another house has been built recently on the site of Charlie Simkin's bungalow, called Railway's End.

Local people connected with the railway in Blagdon [8]

The construction and subsequent daily operation of the railway and the waterworks attracted many workers to Blagdon at the turn of the 20th century. Some settled in the village but others left after their work stint, notably most of those who were recorded in the 1901 census at:

No. 21, Temporary Navvy's Hut – head Richard Wilding, a 41 year old railway foreman from Preston, Lancashire, with sons Richard junior, railway engine stoker, and Thomas, already a railway labourer at the age of 14. Boarders were Joseph Williams and William Field, railway workers, and John Pilifant, railway foreman.
No. 27, Temporary Navvy's Hut – head William Kerslake, railway sub-contractor from Topsham, Devon. Boarders were Frederick Ketch, railway miner from Hatch, Somerset, and Thomas Brooks, railway timberman from Buckley, Northants.

Oliver Oliver has left an impression, perhaps because of his unusual name, but not much is known about his life in Blagdon, where he was known as 'Oliver Twice.' He is first mentioned in the 1861 census as a two-year-old boy, born in Aberavon, Glamorgan, and living in Llanhilleth, Monmouthshire, and son of a coal miner. In the 1881 census, he is lodging with William Richards, a railway engine driver, and his family in Roath, Glamorgan. He is listed as unmarried and a railway engine fireman. By the 1891 census he is living in Hereford and has graduated to a railway engine driver. He is married to Julia, with a son and a daughter. He is recorded in Bristol in the 1901 census, living at 45 Balmain Street, Knowle, with his wife, two sons and three daughters. 'Oliver Twice' was the regular driver on the WVLR in 1924 and he lodged in Blagdon overnight with the rest of the train crew.

Charles Simkin came from Leicestershire and settled in Blagdon with his wife Mary Ann. Charles was born in 1845 (probably) in Hallaton, Leicestershire, and is first recorded in the 1891 census as a journeyman blacksmith, a boarder in his home town. His name has been spelled in a number of ways. In the 1881 census he is

'Charles Simkin or Pimkin', blacksmith, lodger in Bedehouse Row, Oakham Lordshold, Rutland. In the 1891 census 'Charles Simkins' is married and living at Pitsford, Buxworth, Northamptonshire.

According to one source[9], there were three blacksmiths in Blagdon at the turn of the century: the Monk brothers at Street End, Ernest Humphreys beside the George Inn, and Charlie Simkin's smithy down Station Road – *'when the lake was being dug he used to dress the tools belonging to the men working on the lake.'*

For much of their lives, the Simkins lived in Lake Bungalow, a wooden construction with a metal roof owned by GWR[10] next to the station gate, which Charlie unlocked in the morning and locked at night. He was on hand to provide horse-drawn transport as required. He linked Blagdon with other local villages, delivering railway parcels and hauling milk in churns. Annie took in guests and provided teas, so the bungalow was a sort of 'railway hotel'. According to local knowledge, Will Fyffe (1884-1947), the famous Scottish entertainer, stayed in the bungalow when he was in Blagdon for fishing holidays. It is said that there was a bed which could be hoisted to the ceiling, out of the way in daytime – it is perhaps more likely that it folded up to the wall.

Fig 10 – Charlie Simkin in horse and cart in front of his bungalow
(George Symes)

The family is in Blagdon at the time of the 1901 census – 'Charles Simkins' is a blacksmith and Mary Ann, 'Annie', is a dressmaker. The correct spelling is confirmed in figure 10 - on the side of the bungalow is 'C Simkin Refreshment Rooms'.

Mr Chick, the first station master, was listed as such in Kelly's Directories for 1906, 1910 and 1914. He lived in Station House (now Grasmere) in Station Road, a short distance up from the station (fig 11).

Figure 11 – Charlie Simkin's bungalow
Station House is next up the road and the white house Hillside further on.

Mollie Day (née Harrison) was brought up in Station House and had the job of looking after the camp coach. She also attended to the station premises when they were occupied by Downey's sack factory during the Second World War.

Albert Jones was the regular guard, who had his house, 'Hillside', built in Station Road a short way up from Station House (fig 11). He seems to have been well liked, as it is said that passengers would leave money at the Station Hotel, Yatton, for him to have a drink at the end of the day.[11] He moved to Yatton on his retirement.

Gaythorn Hill, principle director of the Hill's ship-building company in Bristol, lived at Hazel Manor, Compton Martin, about four miles from Blagdon station. He is a legend in Blagdon because he used to walk to the station most days to go to work. When he was late he would blow a whistle at the top of Two Trees to delay the departure of the train until he arrived! He was later on some occasions than others because he carried a walking stick with a thistle hoe and if he saw a bull thistle he would be diverted from his path. Two Trees is a mile from the station but high up Hill Road, so it is plausible that a good whistle would be heard at the station in those times when there was little extraneous noise.

Sammy Sampson and Ambrose Carpenter would collect copies of the Green 'Un and the Pink 'Un from the last train on Saturday evenings during the football season. These were the special editions of the *Bristol Evening Post* and the *Bristol Evening*

World respectively, printed on coloured paper, which carried the football results and reports of the games that afternoon. (After being revived for a number of years, albeit on white paper, the Green 'Un is still published but has now (2006) been incorporated as a free supplement in Monday's edition of the *Evening Post*).

Ralph Stone was born in Burrington but lived most of his life in Bristol. He worked on the main lines for the Great Western Railway, starting as a boiler cleaner aged 17 and progressing to Senior Driver at Bath Road Depot. After being blitzed out of his home during the Second World War, he went to live in Victoria Avenue, Redfield. He has a cameo role in the history of WVLR as it was he who drove the last train in and out of Blagdon. According to the official records Arthur Jones was the driver and this has been recorded in books about the railway. It is now revealed that the drivers switched at Yatton so that Ralph could take the last train through the village of his birth (fig 12). While the train was stopped at Blagdon Station, Ralph walked up Station Road to visit his brother Bert's family at Stones Cottage.

Figure 12 – Last passenger train out of Blagdon 12th September 1931
(Veronica Counsell)

As a senior driver, Ralph was chosen to drive Winston Churchill's train, after which he was photographed shaking hands with the great man (fig 13). He also drove the steam engine 'The Bristolian' to pull the Queen's train when she was in the area. 'The Bristolian' is now in the Museum of the Great Western Railway in Swindon. Ralph drove the first diesel locomotive out of Bristol Temple Meads Station. A clock stands on the mantelpiece of his nephew's home in Blagdon inscribed 'B R Stone: Appreciation of 45 Years Service.' There is also a hammer he used to tap the wheels to check they were sound.

Figure 13 - Ralph Stone shaking hands with Winston Churchill c1940 (Stone family)

Following closure to passenger traffic

In the period immediately following the closure to passenger traffic in 1931 there was only one regular goods train in the morning, with additional trains as required. Blagdon station was left completely unstaffed. The regular train delivered coal for the waterworks. At the start of the Second World War it was departing Yatton at 7.30am and arriving at Blagdon at 8.50am, returning at 9.05am to arrive back in Yatton at 10.26am. John Gallop's father Bert had a farm elevator delivered by an 'as required' train during the Second World War.[12] In 1950 the train left Congresbury at 9.15am, arriving at Blagdon at 10.20am.

Pam May was living at Winscombe in 1939-51 and travelled to work in Bristol along the A38 in her Austin 7. She remembers often being held up by what she termed the 'milk train' from Burrington. According to the 1950 timetable, this left Burrington at 10.50am, arriving at the Stop Board at 10.52 to reach Langford at 10.56.[13]

Not surprisingly, the rarely used track became a playground for the local children. Ken Tucker was born in 1929 and Ivan Carpenter in 1927. When they were boys in the mid to late 1930s, they used to play on the track between Lays Lane and Blagdon station, in particular with bows and arrows and air guns. Ken remembers seeing goods trains on the track, but he cannot remember any building on the site of Simkin's bungalow. He assumes it must have been demolished – there was a standpipe.[14] He also remembers Silvey's lorries delivering coal three or four times a day, and the gangers' (or plate-layers' – author) shed by Lays Lane siding made of railway sleepers set horizontally (fig 14). It had a stove on which they used to heat up impromptu meals and drinks.

Figure 14 – A typical plate-layers'
hut at Congresbury
(J Harrison)

Ken Tucker began his life in farming working for Bert Gallop from 1944 to 1947/48, and eventually became chairman of the Mendip Ploughing Society. While working for Alvis Brothers he managed to save his overtime money for one year, amounting to £143. He used £42 to buy a pig house and was allowed by Wills Estate to use the old quarry beyond the end of Lays Lane. After two years he rented some of the disused railway line from GWR. These were his first steps in farming for himself. He bought the first Landrace boar sold on the open market in this country, in Reading, for £246. It was delivered by train, but only as far as Yatton, the branch line being closed. Gilts were bought in to be served by the boar, kept for two months and then sold on. He then became tenant of Blagdon Hill Farm (Hill Farm today), opposite Leaze Lane on the way up to Two Trees, and never looked back.

Ivan Carpenter remembers playing as a boy on the line with Ken, Ken's brother Evan, Tom Russell, Cecil Gilling and others.[15] He did actually ride on a passenger train for a family day out to Weston-super-Mare, but remembers nothing about it – not surprisingly, as when the line closed to passenger traffic he was aged four. In later years his father Charles said the line was bumpy. Ivan does remember taking rides on the mechanical trolley, whose proper use was to transport inspection and maintenance staff. This would be in the mid 1930s. The trolley had a see-saw handle mechanism for two operators. It just needed a push and would then continue in that direction when the handles were pumped up and down. Ivan and Ken used to pick up the trolley behind Blagdon station and propel themselves as far as Bourne Lane, stopping short to avoid detection. He also remembers the plate-layers' hut, but thinks that fires were usually made outside using wood and coal extracted from the piles of ashes left by the firemen. Coal was still being delivered to Burrington station around that time, some of it destined for Nordrach Sanatorium. It was transported to Nordrach in a long wheel-base Bedford lorry belonging to Ted Marsh. Bert Young used to pick up coke from Burrington for the furnaces at Coombe Lodge.

Ivan lived in Grib Lane at the east end of the village, about half a mile from the station. As the daily morning train approached the end of the line to deliver coal for the steam-powered pumps at Bristol Waterworks, the hooter was sounded and Ivan's mother could rely on it to know the time. Ivan also rented about 100 yards of the disused track after Ken. He bought one ginger Tamworth pig, from which he produced a litter of ten piglets. This enterprise only lasted 1½-2 years in the early 1950s, and ended when Ivan became chauffeur to Sir John Wills, a position he kept for 39 years. He could not maintain the feeding regime and he sold the animals in 1953 to Joe Cryer.

The track and station today

Blagdon station has been sensitively converted into a dwelling called Little Halt, keeping the original waiting room almost intact. A gate of apparently standard GWR design was *in situ* in 1976 but has since been replaced (fig 15).

The line of the track in Blagdon parish is still enclosed from Bourne Lane through to Little Halt. Much of the fencing appears to be the original GWR style. Of special interest are the occupation crossings for farm use – small gates to allow the passage of animals and machinery. The gate posts are supported by shaped lengths of railway line, presumably the same as the track itself. These gates were necessary because individual farms had been split by the line, which used 40 acres in total from Congresbury to Blagdon. The land has now returned to multiple owners.

Figure 15 - Gate at Little Halt in October 1976 (author's collection)

There are also two culverts between Bourne Lane and Little Halt which allowed cattle and farm machinery to pass under the line. They are quality constructions, essentially brick with heavy cap stones. The eastern one is in particularly good condition and could be renovated with little effort.

Fig 16 – Rail as gate support near the station (author 2006)

Fig 17 - South side of eastern culvert (author 2006)

Figure 18 - Track today looking west beyond Lays Lane (author 2006)

Figure 19 – Station site in 1948 (Veronica Counsell)

Figure 20 - Station sensitively converted to living accommodation (Veronica Counsell)

Tailpiece

A scheme to rebuild a short section of narrow track near Congresbury was considered in the 1970s. Much of the track way remains but there are obstacles to any reinstatement – notably housing development at Wrington. The stretch in Blagdon parish from Bourne Lane to the station is intact except for a collapsed culvert.

Appendices

1. Examples of other economic features of the railway

The following are extracts from the Draft Order of the Light Railway Commissioners[16].

Stations

No platforms need be provided if and so long as all carriages in use on the railway for the conveyance of passengers are so constructed that the lowest step or footboard is not a greater height than sixteen inches above the level of the ground on the outside of the rail.

Signals

No signals other than those at any junction of the railway with a passenger line of the Great Western Railway need be interlocked with the points.

Home-signals and distant-signals may be worked from the station by wires or otherwise but every signal arm should be so weighted as to fly to and remain at danger on the breaking at any point of the connection between the arm and the lever working it.

The Role of Somerset County Council

While the railway was built economically, efforts were made by all parties to build it to a high standard and its construction was planned and monitored in great detail. W.J. Willcox was Architect and County Surveyor for Somerset County Council. On 17th May 1897 he wrote to William Dunn Esq of Somerset County Council bemoaning the fact that his *'time is limited for Road and Bridge inspecting…'* but outlining his opinions on the railway construction:

'Things the County ought to insist on

1. *That where the railway crosses the main roads – the existing levels and section of such roads shall be maintained and not interfered with.*

2. *That where such crossing takes place – between existing hedges or boundaries – the railway shall be constructed on longitudinal sleepers of adequate scantlings – the rails shall be in section and*

weight similar to an ordinary railway and secured on heavy chairs and bolted to the sleepers. That strong metal guards be placed on the outsides of such rails – that the space between such rails – and lock width of at least 2' 6" on the outside of the rails – be pitched with pennant or hard stone so as to keep the road surface level with the top of the rails – and that such guards and pitching shall be for ever hereafter maintained at the expense of the promoters.

3. *That the gates which will be erected to shut off the railway from the main road at either side shall be of sufficient width, shape and strength… shall have proper bolts and fastenings to keep them in place – to close right across the main road at the time of the crossing of the trains – and that the gates shall be so closed by the company's servants at such time – to open when the train has passed and powers taken to enforce this with "fines"? if the gates are left shut after the train has passed.'*

William Dunn followed up with a letter from Frome, Somerset, dated 25th October 1897, to Secretary, Light Railway Commission, 23 St George Street, London SW:

'Such gates to be opened and closed by the Company's Servants and always opened immediately after the passing of a train. If kept closed unnecessarily the Servant in default should be liable on summary conviction to a penalty not exceeding 40/-.'

However, later W.J. Willcox writes to William Dunn on 28th February 1901:

'I thought it was agreed that the promoters of the railway were not to raise the level of our main road where they cross. The Road Surveyor reports that the contractor has raised our road 1' 6" to 2' 0"' making a very dangerous little rise in what was before a level road.'

In a further letter on 7th March 1901:

'It seems to me the promoters have powers to do what they always wished to do with their plans and the County's suggestions and wishes have been disregarded. We can't stop them raising our road now. There is no clause for the protection of the County in the order… . Is it any use my seeing the Engineer?[17]

3. Map of requisitioned land for the WVLR (see figure 5)

The following is a detailed list of the requisitioned land and the landowners[18] and occupiers coupled with the corresponding field numbers and names recorded on the Tithe Map 1842[19].

Nº = number shown on the plan in figure 5.

Type: A = arable, P = pasture, O = orchard, fp = footpath, d = drove, p = pipes, w = works.

BWW = Bristol Waterworks Company.

TWCC = Trustees of Wrington Congregational Chapel.

SCC = Somerset County Council.

ARDC = Axbridge Rural District Council.

Nº	Type	Field number/name	Owner	Occupier if different
1	A	19 Flow	Sir WH Wills	Joseph Cryer
1a	P/fp	20 Flow	John Henry Spreat	William Young
1b	P	21 Little West Close	Sir WH Wills	Joseph Cryer
2	road	Bourne Lane	SCC/ARDC	Public
2a	P/fp	57 Hunts Paddock	Sir WH Wills	Joseph Cryer
3	A	56 Great Hooks	Sir WH Wills	Joseph Cryer
3a	P/fp/d	55 The Paddock	Samuel Filer	Annie Carpenter
3b	A	58 Ringing Mead	Sir WH Wills	Joseph Cryer
4	P/shed	64 Three Acres	Samuel Filer	Annie Carpenter
4a	P	63 Black Ley part	Samuel Filer	Annie Carpenter
5	P	54 Bushy Close	Samuel Filer	Annie Carpenter
5a	P	65 Middle Mead	Sir WH Wills	Joseph Cryer
6	O	planted as orchard	Sir WH Wills	Thomas Williams
7	A	53 Broad Hooks	Sir WH Wills	Joseph Cryer
8	P	50 Orchard Long Hooks + 51 Long Hooks Paddock	Sir WH Wills	Joseph Cryer
9	P/p	71 Yeo Mead part	Sir WH Wills BWW	Thomas Williams BWW
10	P	73 Middle Mead + 74 + 75 unnamed	Sir WH Wills	Thomas Williams
11	P/p	77 unnamed	Sir WH Wills BWW	Thomas Williams BWW
12	A/p	78+79+part 80 all Leys	Sir WH Wills BWW	Thomas Williams BWW
13	P	76 Bonhill	Sir WH Wills	Thomas Williams

14	P/p	81 Leys	Sir WH Wills BWW	Thomas Williams BWW
15	P	86 Parsons Ley	Rev. Gilbert Lyon	Sir WH Wills
16	A/p	82 Golden Bottom	Sir WH Wills BWW	
17	A	87 Broad Leys + 88	Sir WH Wills	
19	P/p	83 Lower Lays	Sir WH Wills BWW	
20	P/p	85 Hays	Sir WH Wills BWW	
21	A	89	Sir WH Wills	
22	A	90 Leys + 91 Lower Leys + 92 Upper Leys	Sir WH Wills	
23	P/fp/p	84 Uxford	TWCC/BWW	Sir WH Wills BWW
24	P/fp/p	277 Uxford	Samuel Baker BWW	Richard Wilding BWW
25	A	274 Uxford	TWCC	George Edwards
25a	d/lane	Lays Lane	Sir WH Wills/TWCC	Public
26	P	276 Jaddy Ham	Mary Cole Anna Stevens	Joseph William Panes
27	P	273 New Close	Benjamin Panes	William Lyons
28	P	276 Long Paddock	Benjamin Panes	William Lyons
29	P/p	278 Yeo Mead	Benjamin Panes BWW	William Lyons BWW
30	P/w/p	278 Yeo Mead part	BWW	
31		stream	Benjamin Panes	William Lyons
32		stream and pond	Benjamin Panes BWW	William Lyons BWW
33	P	279 Uxford Hill	Benjamin Panes	William Lyons
34	P	283?	BWW	
35	Hut	in 279 Uxford Hill	William Day	
36	Hut	in 279 Uxford Hill	William Cann	
37	Hut	in 279 Uxford Hill	Thomas Hurlston	Richard Wilding
38	P	250 Great Hurst	Mrs Mary Bailey	Morley Gallop
39	P/w	280 Millwood N part	BWW	
40	P	280 Millwood S part	Mrs Mary Bailey	Morley Gallop
40a		Mission Room in 280	Sir WH Wills	
41	P	282 + 281 part Millwood	Mrs Mary Bailey	Morley Gallop
42		Buildings in Millwood	BWW	Pethick Brothers
43	Store	287 Ploddy south	BWW	
44	Works	287 Ploddy south	BWW	
45	P	249 Wood Yeates Garston	Mrs Mary Bailey	Morley Gallop

46	P/w	288 Hurst + 289 Wood Yeates Garston + 281 Millwood part	Mary Bailey BWW	Morley Gallop BWW
48	Works	287 Ploddy south	BWW	
49	Saw Mill	288 Hurst	BWW	
50	Cement House		BWW	
51	P	290 Great Garston	Mary Bailey BWW	Morley Gallop BWW
52	Road	Station Road	SCC/ARDC	Public

Lays Lane (25a) joined the railway at Wills Estate's private siding named after it. The footpath continues on northwards today to Uxford Bridge over the River Yeo – an ancient bridge of uncertain age, the most notable feature of which is one huge stone slab.

Bibliography

B1   Colin G. Maggs, *The Wrington Vale Light Railway* (Oakwood Press, 2004); the fullest account of the railway published to date.

B2   Michael Farr, Robert Lovell, Colin G. Maggs and Charles Whetmath, *The Wrington Vale Light Railway* (Avon-Anglia, 1978)

B3   C.R. Clinker, article in *The Railway magazine* (November 1959)

B4   Michael Farr, 'Light Rails to Wrington', in *Steam days* (issue no.14, July-September 1989

References

[1]   B1, p.22.

[2]   Station Road is often called Station Hill by older residents; there is a house called Station Hill Cottage.

[3]   This is referred to as a shop in B1, p.103, top picture, but there is no memory of this in Blagdon.

[4]   Recollections of John Gallop, life-long Blagdonian.

[5]   Author's telephone conversation, 4th April 2001, with the managing director, whose great grandfather started the Silvey business in 1870.

[6]   Recollections of John Gallop and Ken Tucker.

[7]   This is the subject of an article in volume 1 of *The History of Blagdon*.

[8]   All the information in this section has been discussed at meetings of the BLHS Recent History Group and checked in a telephone conversation with John Gallop, 27th February 2006, except the part about Ralph Stone, which was the result of a conversation with Relton and Grace Stone on 4th August 2006.

[9]   Article in Blagdon parish magazine, May 1978.

[10]   Inland Revenue valuation book for Blagdon, 1910.

[11]   B1, p.22.

[12]   Author's telephone conversation with John Gallop, 27th February 2006.

[13]   Author's telephone conversation with Pam, 24th August 2005.

[14]   Author's conversation with Ken at Blagdon Fair, 29th August 2005.

[15]   Author's conversation with Ivan at his home, 24th February 2006.

[16]   Somerset Record Office Q/RUP/492

[17]   Somerset Record Office Q/RUO/17

[18]   Somerset Record Office

[19]   Tithe map, Somerset Record Office. Copy by Rob Marley in BLHS Archives.

WELLS IN BLAGDON

John Chamberlain

Introduction

As far as is possible the locations of many wells have been checked from the 1883-4 Ordnance Survey and subsequent maps but much information is the result of local knowledge. Because of the disposition of the maps (figs 1- 4) it is not possible to include the location of all known wells and there are instances where tradition suggests that wells should occur but they have neither been located nor recorded.

Wells, Cisterns and Springs

Since early times one of the principal reasons for the continuing existence of the settlement of Blagdon has been the consistent availability of clean water. When, in 1904, the lake first reached its full working level, many Blagdonians were disappointed to find that it supplied water to only eight houses in the village. Whilst very rudimentary 'mains' water from springs above the village had been available before this date, the majority of dwellings in the parish continued to rely on wells for water supplies. One exception in this context was the hamlet of Rickford, served in its entirety by water from the stream flowing from the 'Great Spring' at Rickford Rising. Despite the introduction of standpipes, the lack of a reliable sufficient public mains supply persisted well into the 1920s. Throughout 1921-22 there were complaints of lack of supply and in 1923 the insufficiency was reported to the Ministry of Health.

The wider geology of the area provides the conditions for a local supply of water. Triassic rock layers of Keuper Marl and Dolomitic Conglomerate (Puddingstone) overlie the steeply inclined Carboniferous Limestone Series. The Carboniferous consists of Hotwells Limestone, Clifton Down Limestone, Burrington Oolitic Limestone, Black Rock Limestone and the Lower Limestone Shale. The Devonian lies beneath the Limestones and consists of the Quartzitic Sandstone of the Old Red Sandstone Series.

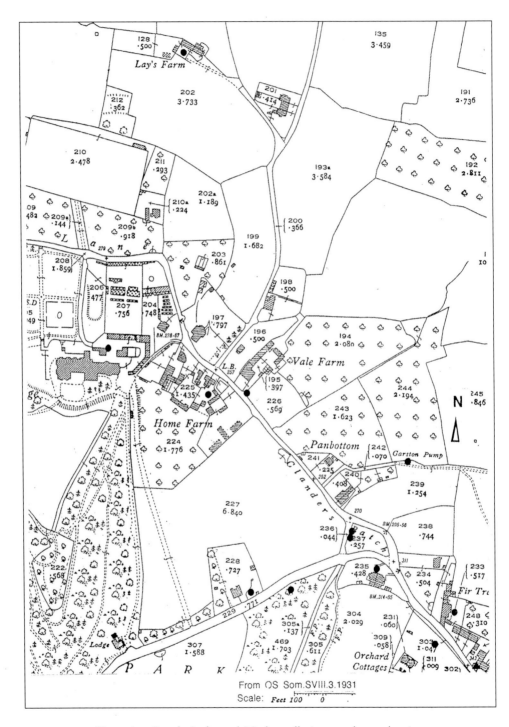

Figure 1 – Coombe Lodge and Menlea well, cistern and sump locations

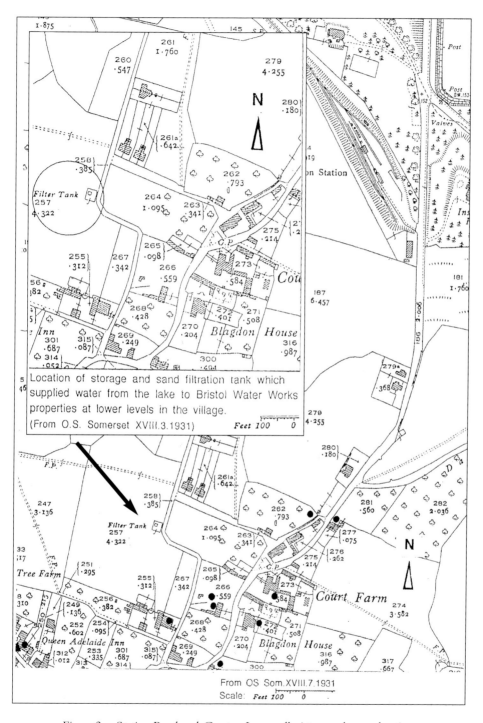

Figure 2 – Station Road and Garston Lane well, cistern and sump locations

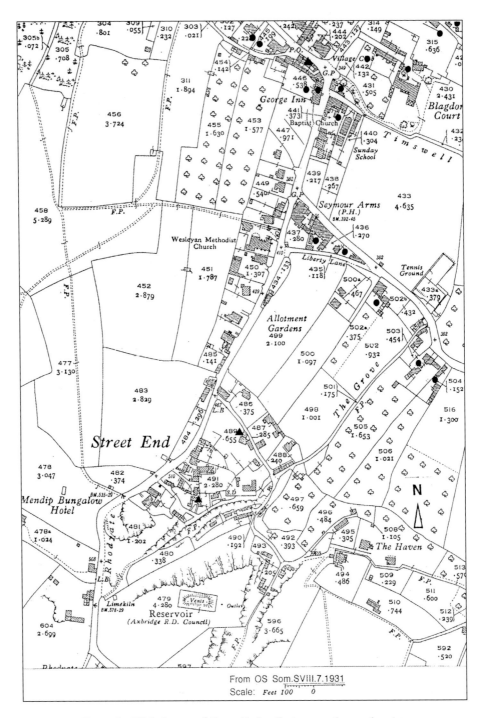

Figure 3 - High Street and Street End well, cistern and sump locations

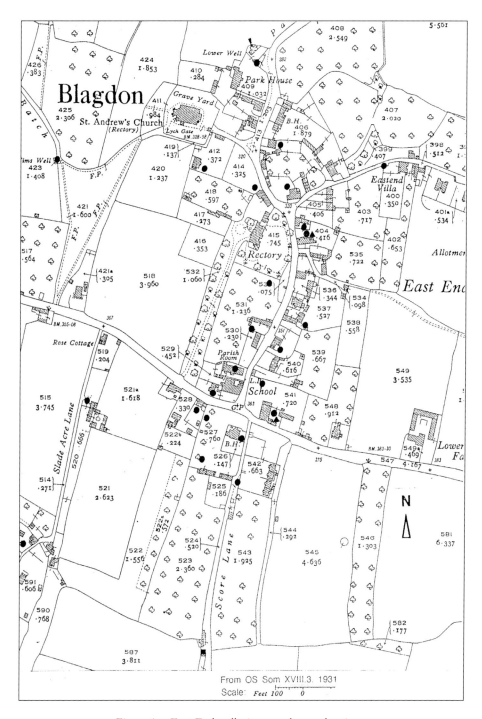

Figure 4 – East End well, cistern and sump locations.

Above the village further springs emerge from the hillside and, unless directly associated with the original village 'mains' supply, either decant into swallets at the boundary between the Lower Limestone Shale and the Limestones, or find a southerly course through the Mendips.

In Blagdon the term 'well' is often a misnomer. The two best known publicly accessible wells, Timsell Well (Timswell) and Lower Well, are in fact cisterns fed by springs, as is Garston Well (fig 6). Two further 'wells', Hanging Well[1] to the east and Squire's Well to the west, are also springs. The farmsteads of Merecombe and Wadley also relied on springs for their water supplies. These springs emerge from the hillside at the boundary between the Dolomitic Conglomerate and the impermeable Keuper Marl, broadly along an east-west line on the 80m contour. They not only provided water but also formed a notional northern boundary to the village below which, historically, little development took place. The underground watercourses which feed the springs also act, in many cases, as the source of water in true shaft wells in the village and these are excavated into the porous Dolomitic Conglomerate.

In addition to their geological structure the Mendips are internationally known for cave systems and associated underground watercourses. It is possible that Blagdon may share such features, of which the springs and wells are a surface manifestation. Another feature of this geological framework is the hard nature of many of the rocks which outcrop throughout the village. It is easy to see why Blagdon relied principally on emerging springs as a source of water supply but more difficult to understand why the village has so many true wells, whose digging required considerable human effort.

Reliance on well water supply generally implies sinking a shaft in which water in the ground collects as a result of natural seepage. In effect the water which collects is still, or standing, water, deriving for the most part from migration of surface water. Although there are undoubtedly 'collection' wells of this type in the village, the majority of well shafts were sunk to depths at which underground running water courses could be exploited. This is not to say that ground water seepage into any shaft could not occur.

To sink, or dig, a well shaft through hard rock with hand tools was a difficult undertaking. Shafts were sometimes no more than a metre in diameter, extending to 1.6/1.7 metres and 15m or so below ground level. Working in such a confined space required considerable physical effort and dexterity. It was obviously not a task to be undertaken unless there was a reasonable certainty of a successful outcome. Before the introduction of electronic devices the skills of a known water diviner, or dowser, may have been employed. To date no reference has been found in the parish records

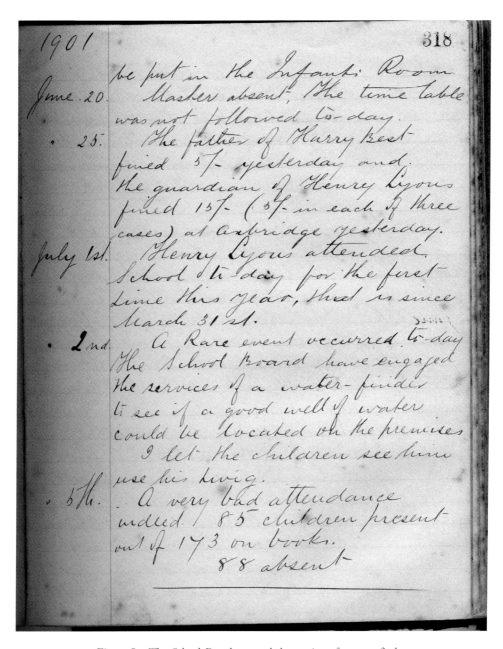

1901

318

June 20. be put in the Infants Room Master absent. The time table was not followed to-day.

25. The father of Harry Best fined 5/- yesterday and the guardian of Henry Lyons fined 15/- (5/- in each of three cases) at Axbridge yesterday.

July 1st. Henry Lyons attended School to-day for the first time this year, that is since March 31st.

2nd. A Rare event occurred to-day. The School Board have engaged the services of a water-finder to see if a good well of water could be located on the premises. I let the children see him use his twig.

5th. A very bad attendance indeed. 85 children present out of 173 on books. 88 absent

Figure 5 – The School Board engaged the services of a water-finder.
Extract from Blagdon School Log (1880-1918)

of such a person resident in the village, but wells in the parish were neither sited nor dug without a degree of certainty. In 1901 the School Board *'engaged the services of a water-finder to see if a good well of water could be located on the premises'* and the children were allowed to *'see him use his twig'²* (fig 5). It is known that, in 1922, Axbridge Rural District Council employed a water diviner to survey and advise on possible further points of supply in the parish.

The construction of wells in the village is varied. The major public 'spring' wells have obviously been subject to various improvements and modifications over many centuries. In earlier times the emergent springs at Timsell and Lower wells probably discharged directly into very basic shallow ponds, or 'dipping' pools, with open channels discharging to a convenient ditch; Garston and Hanging wells also followed this pattern. In the Parish Council minutes for 7th February 1929 there is reference to the posting of notices relating to the filling in of a public dipping pool at Street End, the exact location of which is not recorded. Whether or not this pool was spring fed is not known but the general location suggests that it was a surface collection construction.

The present form of both Timsell Well and Lower Well owes much to the intervention of the Bristol Waterworks Company at the end of the nineteenth century. However, it could clearly be seen, during the relatively recent renovation undertaken by Frank Filer, at the instigation of John Birch, that the lower elements of Timsell Well are obviously of an earlier date. Timsell Well is unusual in directly supplying two ponds in addition to the normal 'domestic' supply. The upper pond is a comparatively recent extension of a much smaller basin. The water was generally acknowledged to be the best in the village and, as recently as the 1920s and 1930s, children would be sent to fetch water from the well from as far away as Street End.

The work at Lower Well has not been of such a complicated form but the enclosed springhead and small ponds formed by Bristol Waterworks were originally enclosed at that time (about 1900) with a white painted picket fence together with a small access gate. This work was reviewed and upgraded by BWW in 1922, by agreement with Blagdon Parish Council.

Apart from determining the site of any well or cistern one of the most exacting considerations of the early well and cistern builders was that relating to the containment of the water collected. In certain cases, especially in the upper sections of well shafts, the exclusion of water often required careful thought.

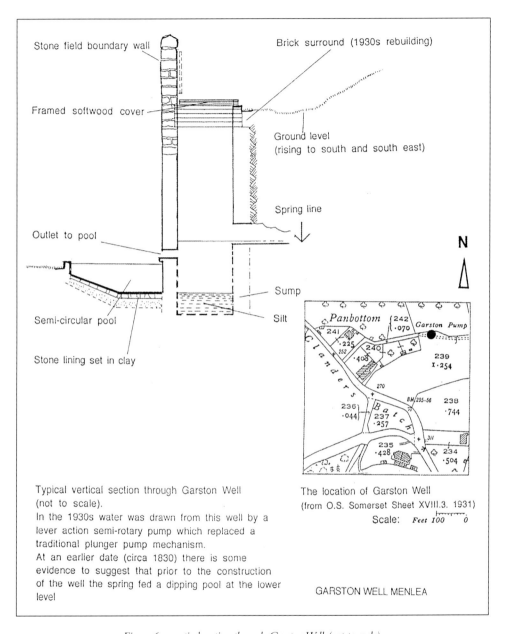

Stone field boundary wall

Brick surround (1930s rebuilding)

Framed softwood cover

Ground level
(rising to south and south east)

Spring line

Outlet to pool

Sump

Semi-circular pool

Silt

Stone lining set in clay

N

Panbottom 242 ·070 *Garston Pump*
241
·225
252 240
·408 239
I·254
270
236 BM/295·56 238
·044 237 ·744
·257
235 234
·428 ·504
Jil

Typical vertical section through Garston Well
(not to scale).
In the 1930s water was drawn from this well by a
lever action semi-rotary pump which replaced a
traditional plunger pump mechanism.
At an earlier date (circa 1830) there is some
evidence to suggest that prior to the construction
of the well the spring fed a dipping pool at the lower
level

The location of Garston Well
(from O.S. Somerset Sheet XVIII.3. 1931)
Scale: *Feet 100* 0

GARSTON WELL MENLEA

Figure 6 – vertical section through Garston Well (not to scale).

133

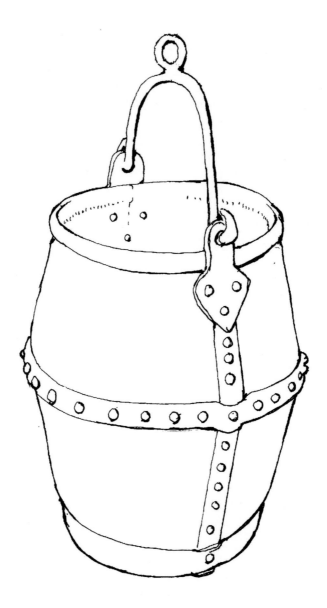

Figure 7 – a well bucket from Sladacre Barn. The shape, tapering to top and bottom, was intended to ensure smooth passage over any projections in the well shaft and as little water spillage as possible during transit. It is possible that this bucket was made by a local blacksmith.
(Illustration John Chamberlain)

In the greatest number of known sites walls and shaft linings were built of hard and relatively impervious local stone in random sizes set in mortar beds. None of the pre-1900 construction appears to have been rendered internally and, given good workmanship, the degree of watertightness achieved depended entirely upon the quality of mortar used. The basic ingredient for sound mortar was 'strong' (hydraulic) lime which produced mortars capable of setting in damp conditions or even under water. Traditionally, limes having this characteristic were available from various kilns across the Mendips associated with hard limestone quarries, such as those at Callow Hill, Shipham, and Batscombe at Cheddar. Within the parish the kiln to the west of Ham Farm was also said to be capable of producing small quantities of 'strong' lime.

Once dwellings were served by a reliable piped supply, practically all the shaft wells in the village were filled and the mouths capped. A typical well structure is demonstrated by that surveyed in 1997 during the renovation of Fir Tree Farm. At that time Mike, a labourer and 'spare time Mendip caver', on the staff of Richard Farmer, builder of Wedmore, was lowered into the well. At the time of his descent, during April, the well was dry, although at other times water was clearly visible at the bottom of the well. A vertical section and notes relating to this well are shown in the illustration (fig 8). Whilst it was not possible to establish how water entered the well, since the bottom two metres was buried in silt, it is reasonable to suggest that this well was dependent on the rainfall maintaining a reasonable water table.

A well of similar construction, but of later date, exists adjacent to the north side of Clanders cottages. The shaft of this well is lined with well set rubble stonework to a depth of approximately 40 ft before entering a deep but narrow natural fissure in the underlying rock, at the base of which there is a water course. Until 1936 this well was complete with its pumping mechanism, which comprised a pump barrel located approximately 35 ft down the well shaft with a series of linking rods and levers operated by the pump handle at ground level. A further pump barrel together with attendant handle was attached to the wall of the house (see fig 9). The whole apparatus was dismantled and removed by Wilfred Gilling, a Coombe Lodge Estate employee, assisted by Gilbert Day, a local resident plumber. This pump system was installed at the time the cottages were built on the instructions of Lord Winterstoke. It was used until the cottages were renovated and extended during the building of Coombe Lodge in 1930–32, at which time mains water was introduced.

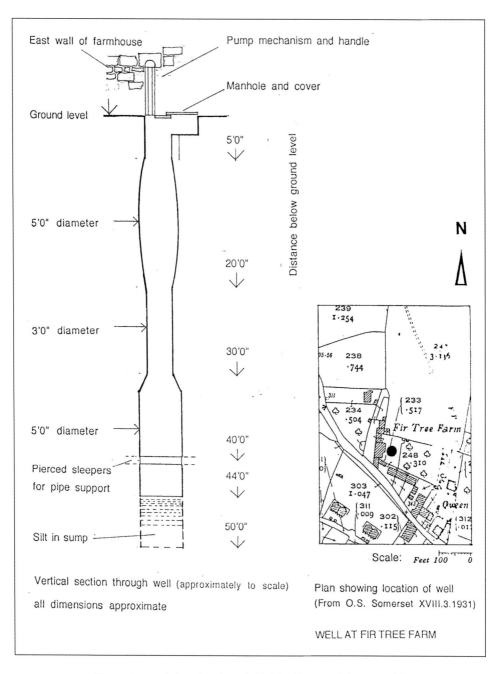

Figure 8 – vertical section through Fir Tree Farm well (not to scale).

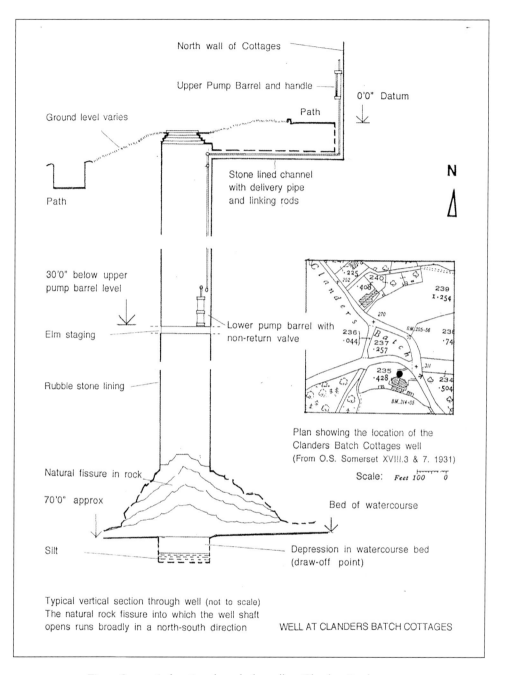

North wall of Cottages

Upper Pump Barrel and handle

0'0" Datum

Ground level varies

Path

Ground level varies

Path

Stone lined channel
with delivery pipe
and linking rods

N

30'0" below upper
pump barrel level

Elm staging

Lower pump barrel with
non-return valve

Rubble stone lining

Plan showing the location of the
Clanders Batch Cottages well
(From O.S. Somerset XVIII.3 & 7. 1931)

Scale: Feet 100   0

Natural fissure in rock

70'0" approx

Bed of watercourse

Silt

Depression in watercourse bed
(draw-off point)

Typical vertical section through well (not to scale)
The natural rock fissure into which the well shaft
opens runs broadly in a north-south direction   WELL AT CLANDERS BATCH COTTAGES

Figure 9 – vertical section through the well at Clanders Batch cottages.
(not to scale)

The only pumping system of this sort (but much fore-shortened) remaining from the 'Winterstoke' era can be seen on the verandah of the house immediately adjoining Mendip Farm Butchers (fig 10). Whether or not this system pumped water from a well or from an underground sump is not known, but it is possible that the Winterstoke rebuilding favours the latter.

Figure 10 – the upper elements of a hand-operated pump system on the verandah of the property adjoining Mendip Farm butchers. That no pump barrel can be seen suggests the presence of a well with a depth of at least 30ft. Water raised by the pump discharged into the sink at the left hand side of the pump standard via a valved pipe.

(Photograph - Julie Chamberlain)

Until the onset of mass production in the Victorian era pumps were not the usual method of raising water from wells. In the domestic situation the normal method was to lower a bucket into the well on a rope or light chain and withdraw it hand-over-hand. In cases when the well water level was at some distance below ground, 'hand drawing' was replaced by a simple drum and crank windlass (see Figure 11).

None of the springs or wells in the village appear to have been enclosed by a well house, a building form commonly found in similar circumstances in the West Country. In practically all known cases well heads were covered either by heavy stone slabs or more simply by wooden lids, some of which were hinged.

Following the introduction of a mains water system, which spread in very piecemeal fashion throughout the village in the first half of the twentieth century, many wells were used as convenient points for the disposal of unwanted rubbish and debris. In the vast majority of cases it was easier to throw things into wells than to take them to the Grib with the attendant necessity of seeking consent from the parish council. There are recollections of articles being thrown into the well of Coombe Cottages at the time electricity arrived, coinciding with the arrival of American troops in 1944.

There is only one recorded instance of a person falling into a well. According to the parish records no cause of death is recorded against the name of Samuel Clements, although it was always believed that he fell into one of the wells at the bottom of the small triangular piece of land adjoining Clanders Batch. These wells presumably served the adjoining cottages and particularly that at the western end of the land referred to.

Whilst Timswell and Lower Well continue to flow (and have not been known to fail in living memory, certainly since 1921) the remaining well springs have fallen into disuse. Squire's Well, noted by Bristol Waterworks as being part of the Rickford Stream catchment prior to 1910, was by 1926 known to rise only intermittently. The well which constantly overflowed across Grib Lane was subject to drainage work by contractors on behalf of Blagdon Parish Council in 1931 and was subsequently lost. Garston Well (fig 6) is covered, but unused.

There were areas in the village where it was neither possible nor realistic to sink wells and where no springs rose. Before 1880, prior to the initial acquisition of property leading to the formation of the Coombe Lodge Estate, these areas were above the southern boundary of the mediaeval village at the head of Score Lane and along Street End Lane. In these locations surface ground water was collected in tanks built into convenient rock faces and from which water was removed by dipping. In some instances roof drainage augmented input from surface water.

Whether or not well water was available, rainwater was an important component of many household supplies until the 1930s. In addition to its well 'old' Coombe Lodge had extensive rainwater collection systems, the water collected being described as 'conserved,' that is, water which had not been contaminated by contact with the ground. This system was used in many of the new Estate houses built in the 1885-1910 period which, when not supplied by a well within the curtilage or by a private main, were connected to large underground sumps to which roof water drained. One such sump was recently discovered in the grounds of Stable Cottage in Street End Lane. Some sumps were obviously of much earlier date. It is likely that constructions now regarded as cellars were in part first used for purposes of water collection and storage. One example was that discovered under the southernmost wing of the Queen Adelaide during major alteration work in the early 1940s.

Figure 11 – the well head at Vale Farm Menlea.
Although a much more sophisticated structure than that at East End Farm general principles of construction, operation and closure remain the same. It is likely that the design for this well head was executed in the offices of Sir Frank Wills, architect and Agent to the Coombe Lodge Estate. (Photograph Julie Chamberlain)

It is extremely difficult to date the original construction of many of the wells with any certainty. Whilst the sites of many wells were noted in original Ordnance Survey records dating from 1883–4, some obviously originate from much earlier times. The majority of the known wells are clearly associated with the three principal subsisting areas of development within the village: East End, West End and Menlea. In the East End some buildings still demonstrate features dating from the sixteenth century, possibly being the rebuilding or extension of earlier structures. At Station Road and in the northern parts of High Street – West End – there is evidence which suggests building activity in the late thirteenth century. Practically all the original buildings in the general area of Menlea have either disappeared or been built over, but where there is evidence of constructions of consequence dating from early times we should perhaps consider the possibility of an equally early date for the construction of any closely adjoining well.

Figure 12 – the well at East End Farm (now Honeysuckle House) in Church Street. Note the rudimentary windlass with crank and chain, the wooden well cover held in place by a large stone and the large slab – possibly of pennant stone – which capped the well construction. Note also that the well head was raised significantly above the surrounding ground levels.

(Photograph Anne and Ted King)

The siting of many wells was dictated by property boundaries and the line of underground watercourses, and attention was clearly paid to the need to avoid contamination.

In farmsteads the well was usually sited at some distance from, and at a higher level than, cattle sheds, yards and steadings. Well heads were often raised above the level of surrounding ground, which would be paved. In many parts of the village ground levels have changed radically and it is possible that some early well heads are now a metre or more underground.

While domestic wells are normally perceived to be located externally in association with a dwelling, there are instances of houses with wells which were accessible from within the house. Whether these wells were originally sited outside and the well incorporated by subsequent property extension or the dwelling was specifically sited to provide an internal source of water, would be an interesting project.

Author's note:

Between 1880 and 1962 the increasing rate of decline in use of Blagdon wells reflects the emergence of several 'mains' water distribution systems and an increasing preoccupation with drainage. There was also considerable argument over the rights to water, especially in the southernmost part of the parish. These matters are an interesting social and technical study which will be the subject of a future article.

John Chamberlain 2006

References and Notes

Bibliography

British Geological Survey. Bristol District. England and Wales Special Sheet – Solid and Drift Edition. National Environment Research Council (NERC 1993).
The Caving Diaries of Harry Savory 1910 – 1921
John Savory - Editor, *A Man Deep in Mendip (1989)*
Peter Jackson, *A History of Mendip Caving (1967)*
Blagdon Parish Council Minutes – SRO\D\PC blagdon 1/2/1

Acknowledgements

Much background information has come from many past and present inhabitants of Blagdon, notably the late Cecil F. Payne and his staff, Mrs Flo Addicott, Frank Filer, Iris Veater and others. I am also grateful to Mell and Roger Kaye and Neil Bentham for details of the Fir Tree Farm well, to Rob Marley who compiled the first overall map showing the location of many wells and standpipes, to Anne and Ted King and to Julie Chamberlain for their invaluable help.

---

[1]   This well was located in Hanging Well Orchard and is recorded in the Parish Council Minutes dated 26 September 1901, p21.

[2]   Blagdon School Log Book 1880-1918, p. 318.

SHOPS AND RETAILERS

Rob Marley

Introduction

The shops of Blagdon have clearly been on the agenda for study amongst local historians for many years. The records held in Blagdon Local History Society's archives show that during the 1960s and 70s they were being discussed by both the Blagdon Historical Society and later the Blagdon Heritage Group. The notes that remain of these researches are sketchy and generally not attributed, but some appear to be made by Mrs Glanville from the recollections of her father George King. Where appropriate these quotes have been included and are identified by being in quotation marks and *italics.*

More recently interest has been rekindled by the Society's *"Recent History Group"* under the chairmanship of John Gallop, the members of which are generally more interested in the last 100 years or so of Blagdon's history. Their method of research is to hold open forums and listen to the recollections of the older people of the village, and while what follows is only as good as people's memories, it is an attempt to record what has been gleaned. John has asked me to set down the gathered information, which will hopefully form the foundation for perhaps more serious and exhaustive research by someone in the future. Dating the periods of the shops and events cannot pretend to be too accurate, but, as there are many reminiscences of shops selling sweets and ice cream, they can be assumed to have been during the childhood of the forum members, that is the 1930s – "the good old days." By the very nature of the forums it has not always been easy to attribute comments and memories to individuals, but where possible they have been credited.

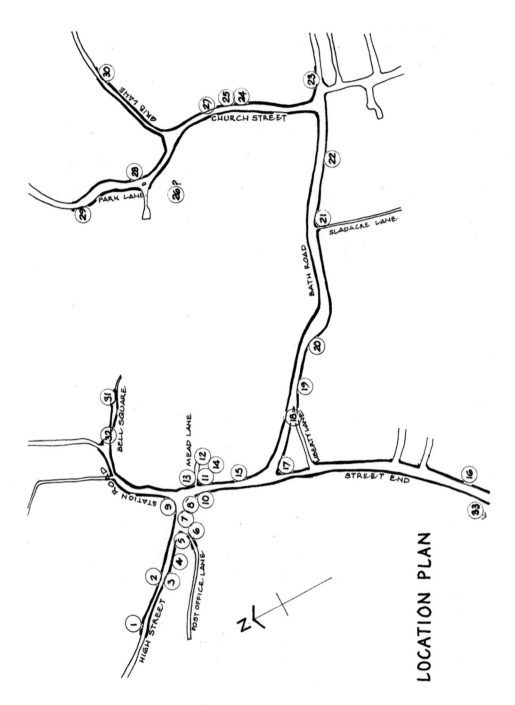

Figure 1 - The location of the shops in Blagdon

1 Fir Tree Farmhouse, High Street

The most westerly of the known shops, being listed in the 1891 census as a pork butcher run by a Mr Carpenter but not trading in 1901. The farm used to make cider, as many did, and at one time it was a public house selling cider rather than beer. In times before that it was a post office, not as we know them today but a place where mail was left for people to collect.

2 Yew Tree Cottage, High Street

Moving along the High Street just to the east of the Queen Adelaide was the Dainty Stores, a wooden structure built in front of the cottage that still stands there today and probably built by Vincent Harris (a carpenter by trade, one of three brothers), and run by his wife. It was not one of the oldest retail outlets in the village, probably beginning in the 1930s and lasting until the 1960s. The Harrises sold sweets, cigarettes, ice cream and groceries and had a number of other enterprises.

After the Harrises came the Vigors. Mr Vigor had an artificial leg and to make his life easier he built a wooden ramp between the cottage and the shop and the local children gave him the nickname of "hump-jump" from the noise he made crossing the ramp.

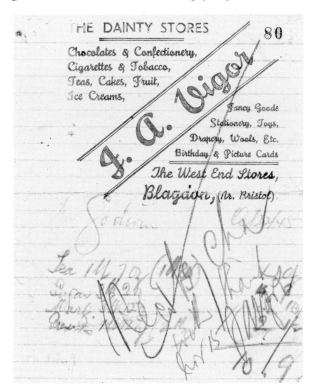

Figure 1 - Vigor Invoice from 1945 BLHS Archive

The next occupants were the Needs, who altered and extended the shop and tried to be one up on the opposition by adding a squirt of raspberryade to the top of the vanilla cornets. At Christmas time a bazaar was held in the front room of the cottage.

Subsequent owners were Mrs Barnes during the 1950s (figure 2) and finally Mr Williams. The concrete base of the shop is still visible today, 2005.

Figure 2 – Barnes Shop near the Queen Adelaide

3 West End House, High Street

On the opposite side of the High Street to Yew Tree Cottage is West End House. The shop was a double fronted building that used to be entered by a short flight of steps up from the street, with another entrance from the east side. Charlie Christen, a Swiss gentleman who married Miss Harris from the Dainty Stores, owned it. He made excellent ice cream and sold sweets and fireworks. At a Recent History Forum held in October 2005 Mary Hibberd recalled that Mr Christen made ice cream wafers twice as big to attract custom from rival shops! The house was used as a guesthouse and had a tea garden and was known as West End Café.

When the Vigors took over the Dainty Stores, a Maltese lady who was probably the wife of Edmund Arthur Vigor ran West End House (Figure 3). During World War II the shop was converted into a private house.

Figure 3 - West End Café & Tea Rooms
(from Duncan Day's collection – copy in BLHS archives)

4 Highfield, High Street

A flat-roofed single-storey extension was built on to the front of the house and used by a branch of the East Harptree Co-operative Society and opened in about 1956. The house was bought from Mrs Harry Cook and managed by Leonard "Skimmy" Currell. It was still trading in 1972 and two people who were known to have worked there were Mrs Parsons and Mr Ebdon who made the deliveries – order on Tuesday, delivery Thursday.

5 Post Office Lane

In 1901 the census records that Benjamin Panes was the owner of the post office, having been a shopkeeper and postmaster in the census of 1891, and the sub-postmaster was John Nelson working with his wife Louisa. It operated as a post office, grocery and drapers, with the grocery on the left of the entrance, the drapery on the right and the post office up some steps towards the rear.

May Whittam, talking about her memories, said, '*The Post Office, smaller then and with no big windows, sold nearly everything. It was a drapers and grocers, and where you buy stamps now there was a marble topped counter for pork and bacon – Mr Nelson kept his own pigs*'.

Subsequent postmasters were Frank Light, Coles, Spires (who introduced toys and fancy goods instead of food), Welford and finally Pauline Beasley, who, with her late husband John, sold the business in August 1995, just three months short of its centenary as the post office. During their occupation John discontinued selling groceries and vegetables and introduced knitting wools and greetings cards.

Eddy Hasselder, who owned the Stores, bought the business and the post office business was transferred there. Since closure as the post office the premises have been used as an office facility and currently, 2005, "Body & Soul", a health and beauty parlour.

The late Pete Ryley, local character and one time postman and fireman, was a sergeant tank commander during World War II and his good friend was the fiancé of a girl in the village – Frances, daughter of the postmaster Frank Light (Figure 4). His friend was killed in action and Pete came to Blagdon to break the news and ultimately stayed and married her.

Figure 4 – Frances Light with her mother and postman Phil Atwell

6 "Cobblers", High Street

The building was originally the butcher's house and its first use as a shop was when it was converted into an estate agent's office – Osmond Tricks, later changed to Allen and Harris. For a short while it was used by a finance company and then taken by Andrew Addicott, who named it "Cobblers" and operated as a newsagents and tobacconist having moved from Ash's in the High Street. Carole Fear continued the business for a while, followed by Mike Loveless, who ran it as a gun and country sports shop. It is currently (2005) "Cobblers Collectables," a dolls house shop with Rod and Di Mills.

7 Mendip Farm Butchers, High Street

The census shows that the Ball family, who came from Marshfield in Gloucestershire, were in residence in 1901 with Enos Ball, his wife Susan and children Louise and Arthur. Enos, the second youngest, was apprenticed to a blacksmith in his youth and when asked by his boss about his ambitions after finishing his time he said he would never work for another man as long as he lived – and he never did. First he bought a baker's shop and later the butcher's shop complete with slaughterhouse at the rear (Figure 5).

Figure 5 - Arthur setting out on his round in 1905, taken from the book On the road, *by G. Perryman Ball, telling of their farming life in Mendip Farm, Charterhouse, and their emigration in 1923 and subsequent life in Australia.*

Nora Day, writing her memoirs in the Blagdon parish magazine between 1979 and 1983, had memories of Mr Ball.

'One winter men dug a tunnel on the Mendips and Charterhouse through the snow for the butcher and baker's horse and cart to get through to the customers, altho' the roads were rough. I can remember Butcher Ball's horse falling down at the cross roads in spite of having frost nails in his shoes. The poor horse skinned his knees, Butcher Ball led his horse back home and left the cart with meat in it at the side of the road until he got help to take it home'.

The Wigleys, who were related to the Ball family by marriage, bought and continued to run the butchers. The business passed to Reg Wigley, who was a keen footballer and had trials for Bristol City. He died fairly young but his widow, helped by Bill Lyons, carried on trading. Bill, whose family came from Long Ashton, had worked for Reg and had bought a shop in Ubley which he ran in competition to his son Roy, who looked after the shop in Blagdon. Roy and his son John then continued the business, as John still does today.

John Gallop remembers the butcher making deliveries both mid-week and at weekends, and cutting up the meat on the floor of the van.

8 Ash's, High Street

The census of 1901 shows Robert Ash, boot maker, on the premises with a wife and their two sons, Stanley and John Vernon.

In later years steps entered the shop from the High Street and they sold ice cream, sweets and Vantas ("Don't have a thirst, have a Vantas"), a soft drink made on the premises. Later still, Vernon Ash and his wife Dolly ran a shoe shop and sold threads and cottons. After the Second World War Vernon returned as a boot and shoe repairer (Figure 6) (soles and heels, 5 shillings [25p]), working from an adjoining workshop fronting the road. Mrs Ash senior made wonderful ice cream from milk supplied by the Gallops' farm. The ice cream was made in a wooden tub with a steel lining and a mixture of ice and salt in the cavity, churned by turning a handle on the top.

Figure 6 - Vernon Ash
from a photograph in John Gallop's album
(copy in BLHS archives)

After a long period of being vacant the shop was taken by Andrew Addicott, who reopened it as "Cobblers" selling pet food, DIY materials, sewing materials, coffee beans (ground on the premises if desired), as well as ice cream and sundry other items. Latterly Andrew ran the news-agency business from the premises when Cecil Sampson retired from business.

9 The Village Club, High Street

'Was the site of a butcher's shop in 1890'.

10 Rent House, High Street

'There was a shop selling groceries where Lake View (Rent House) is'.

Lake View was a restaurant for a while, owned by Vincent Harris of the Dainty Stores, and the counter was still in place when it became the Wills's estate office. For unknown reasons there is an extremely large cellar under the building.

Figure 7 - Lake View from a photograph in George Symes' album
(copy in BLHS archives)

11 The Stores, High Street

Occupied by the Taylors in 1901, trading as W.J. Taylor. Taylor senior worked in Sandford and son Alan ran the store in Blagdon (Figure 8). Alan decided to change the rules and not open on Saturday afternoons, but following a visit from his father one Saturday the decision was hastily reversed. They operated a full general stores selling paraffin, methylated spirit, barbed wire, chicken wire and poultry feed as well as groceries and a drapery.

Figure 8 - The Stores in Taylor's day (from the BLHS Archive)

In 1910/11 the Redwood family from West Harptree took over the premises and ran the stores in exactly the same way. Home deliveries were regularly made, with Mr Redwood visiting his customers on his Excelsior motorcycle and taking orders for delivery the following day. In the early 1930s deliveries (pastries, fancies and slab cake) were made to Charterhouse three times a week in a Ford van. It was a 1913 Model T Ford, the chassis being provided by Jack Roberts and the van built by Fred Watts in his workshop in Liberty Lane. The lintel over the opening to what is now the sorting office was cut to allow for the extra height of the delivery lorry. The problem was discovered when the new van drove in loaded with potatoes and was too high to get out when it was emptied. Bert Shipsey drove the lorry and continued to do so until he was 75 years old.

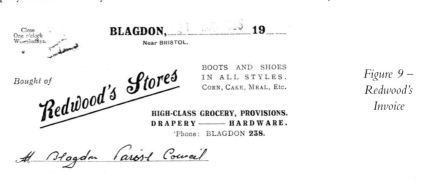

Figure 9 – Redwood's Invoice

Figure 10 - The Stores in Redwood's day (from the BLHS Archive)

The business expanded to include Redwood Cottage in Mead Lane and the Shipsey family lived there until moving to a larger property on the Coombe Lodge Estate. Harry Addicott then lived in Redwood Cottage and Mr Redwood promised that he could live there for the rest of his life.

When E.J. Cole and Sons, the local bakers, bought the premises in 1945 this promise was honoured and the cottage was not included in the sale. The shop was managed by Donald Cole, son of 'Baker' Cole, who began trading on the 24th March 1945 and did not retire until 1972. Half the premises formed a grocers shop and the other half, at a higher level and entered from a separate door from the road, a drapery which 'fitted out' families with all their clothing needs. Donald Cole would collect anything not in stock from Bristol. He always believed he could supply anything, hay barns and pigpens included, "but not second hand coffins!" His proud boast was that he sold a car and a hay barn to Tom Pearce at Middle Ellick Farm and, although Cecil Cole from Robert's Garage originally went to take the order, Pearce insisted on seeing Don.

During Donald's tenure the drapery business gradually declined, the premises were levelled through and the two entrances reduced to one. The shop fronts were enlarged and the business became groceries and household provisions only, and home deliveries ceased.

In 1972 the business was sold to Mr Shadbolt, a senior salesman for Vauxhall

Commercial in Bedford, and then in turn to Derhams, Hasselders, McMillans and currently, 2006, Johanna and Graham Brown, who have reintroduced home deliveries.

12 Beech Croft, Mead Lane

Used to be called Mead Cottage and was a subsidiary of Redwood's selling china and linoleum.

13 Beech Cottage, Mead Lane

Miss Hallen leased Blagdon Court and ran it as a mental nursing home with her younger companion Alex. She was a very good nurse but a poor manager and as a result the nursing home failed. For a short time they made and sold toffee in Mead Cottage.

14 Cottage next to Baptist Chapel, Mead Lane

'Mr Joe Saint built a brick shop in the yard for Gilbert Lyons as a butcher's shop.'

15 Sovereign Cottage, High Street

Mary Ann Filer ran a shop and general stores from here selling sweets and other things from the room on the right of the front door. The young men of the village used to gather there in the evenings to play cards.

Unfortunately, at about 7 o'clock one morning in 1923, the building caught fire and the late Bett Shaw had vivid memories of the day. *'Mary had been playing cards around the big fireplace on a Sunday afternoon – the fire may have been started by a cigarette'*. The fire pump was hitched to the back of Wills' lorry and towed up from its store in Coombe Lodge to fight it, but because the council had tipped a load of gravel over the hydrant they had to shovel it away before they could get any water. A neighbour, Clifford Skillman, was the first in the house and rescued Mary Ann and was awarded a certificate by the Society for the Protection of Life from Fire. Bett remembers that, *'Money had been stored in various places, including biscuit tins and sweet jars. There is a story of her shouting "What about my drawers?" She was referring to the money put away in them. After Sunday school I would search the ruins and pick up pennies, this went on for years. Whenever a black coin turned up they would say, "she's been round Aunt Mary's".'*

Joan Lyons also tells of the event. *'Then came the surprise – money started rolling from all over the place, a bag of golden sovereigns fell down the chimney, rolls of pound notes were found behind the pictures on the wall, a cocoa tin was found full of melted gold coins. Old blue sugar bags were stuffed up the chimney full of money. They say a box of silver coins took four men to carry to the cellar of the house next door. As the house burned the fire hose was washing money out the front door and down the path. A plank was put across the gate to stop the money rolling into the road. The local police found it impossible to collect all the money – the spectators were pushing it into their boots as fast as they could. Afterwards villagers were seen digging the front garden and leaving with their pockets bulging. Several new motorbikes were seen around the village afterwards and the locals would say "There goes Mary Ann's money." Apparently she used to lend money, mostly for the calf trade – her interest rates must have been rather high.'*

The shop was later taken by Mrs Frank Cryer. The Cryer family were farmers, brother George being a tenant of Ridge Farm and brother Norman living in Sovereign Cottage. The shop was running as a general stores in the 1930s.

16 Lantern Cottage, Rhodyate

Known as Rhodyate Stores and run by Jacob Lyons and his wife Sally, known as "Mrs Weighfinger" from her habit of holding her finger under the weighing pan.

Figure 11 - Mrs Lyons outside her shop (from the BLHS Archive)

Subsequently run by the Brewers, Bill Brewer delivered TVO (tractor vaporising oil) to the local farmers, who were dependent on him for the deliveries, and he continued to deliver during the Second World War. Next came the Titcombes and then Arthur Lake. Mrs Lake sold and made ice cream and rock cakes between 1954 and 1958.

The current owners of Lantern Cottage (Jenny and Duncan Day) believe that a barber operated from part of the premises, as there is a sliding hatch still in existence that was believed to have been used to summon the next customer. A barber named Hunt used to operate from the cottage above Lantern Cottage.

17 The Seymour Arms

'The back of the Seymour Arms was a bake house and the baker's name was Thomas Brunt.'

18 Cottage at junction of Liberty Lane and Bath Road

Tom Brunt was a cabinetmaker who trained with a Yatton furniture maker and while at Yatton he made wooden propellers for aircraft and, during World War II, Mosquito fighters.

He lived in this cottage with his widowed mother who, with her late husband, had been licensee of the George public house. He tried opening an antique shop but he was not very successful, often working away in Cheddar. It didn't last long as a shop and he switched careers to the Civil Service.

Figure 12 - The shop front is still evident on the Bath Road frontage.

19 The Old Bakery, Bath Road

Originally used as a bakers by the Hemmens family and taken by E.J. Cole & Sons in 1928, who started baking on the premises in 1930. Edward 'Baker' Cole started his working life in the early part of the 20th century and in 1911 was making deliveries in a horse drawn van with the help of one boy. When he was approaching retirement in 1959 he had three motorised vans but was still working into his 70s and getting up at 4am each morning. Bread was delivered extensively around the area and, as in many other villages, the ovens were opened to the villagers at Christmas time to allow them to cook their turkeys, geese and joints that were too large for domestic ovens.

Iris Veater, writing of her wartime wedding in 1943, has fond memories of the baker: *'Mr Cole — the village baker — always tried to help people getting married and provide something extra if possible…. His meagre ration of dried fruit, fat, sugar etc. was used to make a large slab cake which he cut into small pieces to sell to as many customers as possible according to how many food coupons they could spare… but if there was a wedding, or perhaps a christening, he would cut a slightly larger piece. He made a substitute marzipan using soya flour and put a very thin layer over the cake…then he made a fondant icing… again not being able to spare much sugar or egg white… but because the strange "yellowy" colour of the marzipan would show through the thin white icing he used a drop of cochineal and so I had a very pretty SQUARE PINK WEDDING CAKE… beautifully displayed on a lovely pre war silver cake-stand. I was absolutely delighted with the result… many brides weren't half so lucky and had to make do with a "cardboard" cake which was placed over a piece of plain cake or sponge.'*

Figure 13 - Baker Cole
Photograph from the BLHS Archive

After the closure of the bakery the name was changed to "Little Acorns" and a small shop operated from one room. Later the porch was built and incorporated into the shop. Ann Smith later ran a jewellery and gift shop.

20 Grove Cottage, Bath Road

The business was known as "Sampsons," and Mr Sampson, nicknamed 'Boots', although an invalid, managed to cut people's hair from his bed — they knelt for a haircut. Between haircuts he drank from a flagon of draught beer which he kept by his bed. The business, primarily a newsagents but including haircutting, was inherited by his son Cecil ('Sammy') and wife Anne and they also sold sweets, chocolates and cigarettes and if required would order books.

21 Sladacre Cottage, Bath Road

It used to be called Rose Cottage, and Wilf Saint who lived there built a shop in the east corner of the garden fronting the Bath Road. A bricked up shop front is still visible. Wilf ran a saddle making and harness repair workshop and also mended boots and shoes and made ladies' leather holdalls and handbags. Vernon Ash and Albert 'Ab' Green worked with him for a while.

Figure 14 - The bricked up shop front in 2005

22 School Farm, Bath Road

'Bath Road Stores built by William Wood c 1898.'

The shop was known as "Willy Wood's" and run by a man of that name. A rather reclusive individual, distinguished by his white beard, he only opened the shop once a year to sell apples. He made it his business to walk every footpath in the village once a year to keep them open, even knocking on the door between Stone's and King's Cottages to ask to be let through. The shop window is still evident and fronts the dining room of today's bed and breakfast business.

E.J. Cole & Sons rented the shop in 1951, the owner at that time being Reg Edwards. Reg cleared the shelves of stock from World War II and Donald Cole ran the shop for six or seven years.

It was then taken by Horace Gooding, followed by Denis Silburn for just under a year and then Wilf Bere, who had come from the Blagdon branch of the East Harptree Co-op. They all ran the shop as a general store and after closure various hairdressers used it, the last being "Wavelengths" run by Stephanie Truman.

23 Gilcombe House, Church Street

'A bake house from 1850 or earlier.'

The shop was built on to the house on the Bath Road side and was a bakery run firstly by the Plentys, then Summers and Coles, continuously until Cole moved to the Bath Road bakery in 1928. The school dentist used the premises before the Second World War.

A Mrs Derrick moved in and ran the shop as a general store and sweet shop. More recently it has been an antique shop, a small art gallery run by Delta Hartnell, a small gift shop run by Ted and Dorothy Nugent who sold the premises, not the house, to estate agents Durston & Sons, later Bristol & West.

The building is now in the ownership of the occupants of Gilcombe House, and still retains its shop front.

24 The Upper Barton, Church Street

The Upper Barton is on the site of the barton (farmyard) of Hannah More House.

During the 1920s Jim Best had a fruit and vegetable shop in the outbuilding running parallel to Church Street – now a solid wall on the northern side of the pair of white doors.

The current owners (John and Jackie Chamberlain) believe that the barton outbuildings were converted into a dwelling in the early 1930s. In 1966 the cottage included a very simple shop and the blocked up doorway was still visible and the steps to the road still in place. The block walls under the large windows still sloped towards the road, presumably having formed the bases of sloping display boards.

25 Hannah More House, Church Street

Part purchased in 1745 by Richard Spurlock, a butcher, who held it until August 1758 when it was sold.

'Hannah More House was a butcher's shop and slaughterhouse.'

26 Rose Cottage, Church Street

'Rose Cottage near Church, tailor's shop kept by Mr & Mrs Tossell.'

27 Cherry Trees, Church Street

Known as Miss Durbin's or Durban's, who ran it as a grocery store and sweet shop. George Tricks remembers, '*she sold sweets – sherbet fountains and gobstoppers. These last changed colour as they were sucked and the children took them out of their mouths from time to time to see if they had changed.*'

It was then taken by the Derhams – no relation to the Derhams in the Stores in the High Street. A Mr Davidson was the last to run the shop in this way and in about 1968 Margie Brett selling Galt toys took it. Next came Mrs Scone and then Myra Gay, who both ran it as a gift shop until its closure and return to residential use in the 1980s.

28 The Old Saddlery, Church Street

The shop was adjoining the cottage and fronting Church Street. It belonged to Ambrose Carpenter, known as 'Buff', who was very deaf and latterly had very poor sight. He was a harness maker by trade but sold and delivered the morning papers – the *Bristol Times and Mirror* (now the *Western Daily Press*). On Saturdays, because the round was larger, he made the deliveries by motorcycle and sidecar. George Tricks sometimes accompanied him and they rode out to West Harptree to leave the papers in the pubs or post office for collection.

29 Spring Cottage, Church Street

'*At "Lower Well" Ted Brunt had a shoemaker's shop that made boots for farmers.*'

'*Mr Brunt lived who made boots for local folk (also leggings).*'

30 Little Court, Grib Lane

'*Little Court, Ambrose Carpenter's old house was the shop built in front (saddlers and newspapers). There was rivalry between Carpenter's and Sampson's – Pony and Trap versus bicycle.*'

'*There was another tailor's shop at East End House, now Little Court, where the tailor was Mr Harris.*'

31 Clennon House, Bell Square

In 1901, John Davis with his wife Fanny and eight children occupied it. He was a farmer and butcher and the premises were a butcher's shop and slaughterhouse. At the rear was a veal stage where the young calves were kept in the dark on a raised bed of faggots and fed only milk. The shop front is very much in the same position as the present front door, that is in the south-west corner.

During the 1920s it was used as a fish and chip shop under the proprietorship of 'Steady Eddie' and they delivered to Street End and Rhodyate, often after the pubs closed and sometimes as late as mid-night as testified by the striking of the Coombe Lodge clock. While the frying was taking place they liked to listen to music and there was constant running up and down stairs to wind the gramophone.

Figure 15 - Bell Square and footpath to Clennon House

From the BLHS Archive

32 Purligog, Bell Square

There were four cottages in Bell Square and the shop was in half of Purligog. Albert and Lucy Westcott sold lemonade at 3d (about 1.25p) with a halfpenny back on the bottle if the marble was still intact. The lemonade was kept on shelves in the passageway running from the front to the back of the house.

The current owner is Andrew Addicott, whose father was a joiner and undertaker who had his workshop in the building in the garden at the rear.

33 Charterhouse School

The Charterhouse Centre was the schoolhouse and the little shop was on the right hand side of the front door and run by Percy Walters. Percy was the husband of the teacher, made his living betting on horses, and liked to collect and sell 'ancient remains' from the mineries. He was still operating during the Second World War selling cigarettes, chocolates and mineral waters, often to the airmen based on Blackdown.

Conclusion

Figure 16 lists the premises described above and includes, where known, an indication of the length of time each business was operational. The graph clearly illustrates that the number and spectrum of retailers in the village has greatly diminished from their hey-day when there were over thirty to the four remaining today.

Figure 16 - Shops longevity

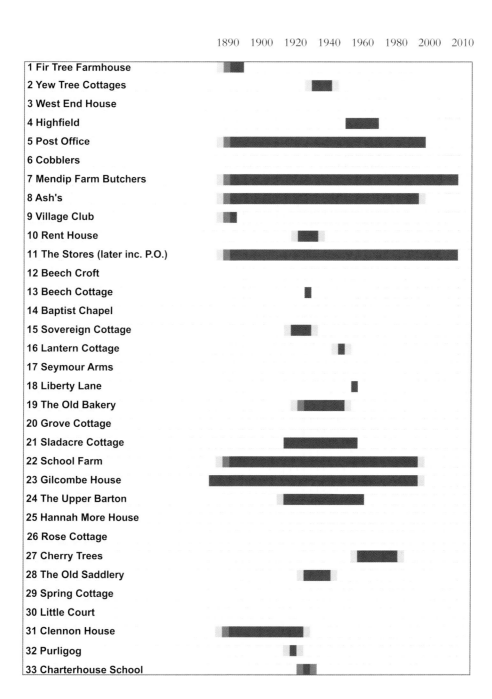

THE BLAGDON BRANCH OF THE BRITISH LEGION
1930 – 1979

Byron Winter

In putting together this account my thanks must go to Les Barnes, Branch Secretary (apart from other responsibilities) 1958-1969 and 1974-1979, for obtaining the appropriate records from Area Headquarters. His help in reviewing the various drafts was invaluable. Sadly, in April of this year (2005) Les passed away before the final version went to print.

At a meeting of ex-Servicemen held in the Parish Room on 19th November 1930, the Blagdon Branch of the British Legion was formed. Presiding was Dr Pineo, who was chairman of the Churchill Branch, from which many Blagdon men were leaving to form their own association.[1] He was supported by a Mr H.C. Turner and Rev. E. Marriott.[2] By the end of the meeting, and with considerable enthusiasm, the first officers were elected.

Rev. E. Marriott	Chairman
Mr. B.J. Gallop	Hon. Treasurer
Mr. S.G. Starr	Hon. Secretary

The following were elected on to the Executive Committee: L. C. Atwell, M. Fraser, F. Cryer, W. Monk, R. Pearse, F. Monk, and H. Young.

Blagdon Village Club was to be the headquarters, annual subscription 2/6, payable in one amount. Dr Pineo announced that he would present the branch with a Legion standard (Fig. 1), soon to be covered in white linen, donated by Mrs Marriott. Later Mr Godwin presented a Union flag.

The standard was dedicated at St Andrew's on Sunday December 14th, 1930. The parish magazine of January 1931 noted that, '*Ex-Service men of Blagdon supported by goodly contingents of comrades from Wrington, Banwell, Churchill and the Chew Valley, headed by their Standards, marched from the centre of the Village to our Parish Church to worship God in common and to witness the dedication of the Standard of the Blagdon branch of the British Legion. It was a stirring sight and an inspiring occasion .... At the end of Evensong the Standard was placed, for safe keeping, in the Memorial Chapel. I can scarcely say what a very great pleasure it was to welcome on this auspicious occasion, Sir Vernon Wills, who commanded the Parade, and Dr. Pineo, thro' whose generosity our branch of the Legion has obtained its Standard.'*

And here, in the chapel, it was kept until paraded by Mr T. Saint, who had been duly elected the first Standard Bearer.

Figure 1- British Legion Standard -
Blagdon Branch. Memorial Chapel, St Andrew's Church, Blagdon

Soon new members were joining, and the names recorded attending the December meeting of that year were Messrs G. Walters, C. Davis, F. Light, A. Filer, W. H. Lyons, E. F. Filer, P. Atwell, M. Fraser, F. Hollier, H. Rayson, F. Cryer, J. Skitmore, H. Villis, E. Avery, R. G. Lyons, R. Pearse, T. Saint, V. Ash, F. Higginson, R. Baber, W. Harrison, F. Monk, H. Young, G. Sherbourne, E. Carpenter, K. Harvey, G. Light, A. Lyons, A. Baber, the Chairman, Treasurer and Secretary.

Times were not easy, especially in the early 1930s. The crisis of the General Strike had come and gone but many branches of the British Legion were reporting members falling on hard times, with the obvious effects upon their families. It was one of the prime concerns of the officers to look after their members when money was short. Here the work of the benevolent committees was vitally important, and Blagdon was no exception. Many of today's Welfare State provisions were not in place, and so to a great extent the British Legion exercised a social responsibility to those members affected by redundancy, short time, ill-health or bereavement.

In order to swell the funds, including those of the benevolent account, a series of whist drives and dances were planned. Unfortunately the organisation of the first of these, including the Annual Dinner (to be held at the George Inn but later changed to the Village Club), was thrown into turmoil by the unexpected death of Sir Vernon Wills.

As Vice-President of the South Western Area, Sir Vernon was active in the movement, and the minutes record that, '... *the Legion as a whole and the Churchill and Blagdon Branches in particular had lost one who had their interests very much at heart'*. The funeral took place at St Andrew's Church on 1st February 1931, and only then on 28th February 1931 did the inaugural dinner take place.

With the branch now established, the elected officers went about their duties. Conferences and rallies were attended, with enthusiastic delegates reporting back to meetings. Correspondence with area and head offices was read out. On many occasions this proved to be important when applying for grants from various Legion relief funds. Giving an idea of the emotions of the time, the report by several members who attended a Bath rally on 1st June 1931 stated, '*There were 20 Branch Standards on Parade, and approximately 800 men. The band and bugles of the Somersets headed the march to the Pump Room. As there was a little time to spare before the meeting commenced the band played "Tipperary" and "Pack up your troubles", and the chorus went remarkably well'*.

Regarding the movement as a whole, the rally was told that in 1921 there had been 191 branches in the south west area but now, in 1931, there were over 500 and the number was still growing. Mr Kennedy, the region organiser, appealed to the present members, during this the 10th anniversary of the formation of the Legion, to get all ex-servicemen to join. This resolution the Blagdon branch took to heart.

Of course, the most significant event during the year was the service of remembrance. In 1931 it was proposed by the chairman to hold this on the Sunday following November 11th. The parade was to muster at the Club at 6pm and march via the main road to the church headed by the branch standard. Mr Whittam and Mr Frise were deputed to lay the wreath, Dr Melvin to be Officer Commanding parade and Mr Atwell Commanding Officer. For some reason the reading of the names of the fallen was dispensed with.[3] This was to be the format for some years, but being augmented with the services of a bugler who would sound 'The Last Post' and 'Reveille' to mark the two minutes silence. In 1933 there was the addition of a morning service held at the Baptist and Wesleyan chapels in alternate years. It was only after the arrival of Rev. Neep in 1958 that the main service changed to observe the now usual 11 o'clock period of silence. Also in the early years there were area services of remembrance where members were invited to attend.

In the village, Earl Haig's Poppy Appeal was organised by Miss Daisy Wood (Fig. 2), and out of recognition of her services the Blagdon branch voted her as an honorary member. For many years she was to continue in this and also to participate in the business of the association, regularly attending the monthly meetings.

Figure 2 - Daisy Wood

The branch appears to go from strength to strength. New members joined and by April 1932 there was the intention to contact all ex-servicemen who were still outside the movement and encourage them to join.

Many of the new members who came along were not against shouldering office, and in particular two names ought to be mentioned. Firstly, it was proposed at the second AGM on November 13th 1932 that Lady Wills be asked to accept the Presidency of the branch. (Lieut. Colonel C. L. Estridge, DSO, was asked to be Vice-President.) By the next meeting in January 1933 Lady Wills had replied and expressed her willingness to take on the office. It was a post she was to hold for the next 22 years. In her Presidential Address given at the 4th AGM in October 1934 she thanked the branch for the honour, pointing out, '*That her qualifications so far as service went, were such as made her quite eligible for that position. She had served, as a nurse, in a Military Hospital, from July 1916 to July 1919*'. This prompted applause from those present. It was not until the early 1950s that Lady Wills relinquished this post. In that time she showed great interest in the branch, invariably attending AGMs and being involved in fund-raising.

At the monthly meeting of April 29th 1933 a prospective new member made his application to join the branch and was duly elected. He was Mr H.R. Headford,[4] headmaster of the local primary school. In the years to come he was to be a staunch committee member, especially in the troubled years in the latter part of the decade and during World War II. In October 1934 he became Treasurer and in the dire times of 1940 was voted Treasurer and Secretary, positions he was to hold until 1948 when the latter responsibility was taken over by Mr N.M. Fisher.

As the 1930s progressed the elected officers of the Blagdon British Legion fulfilled their responsibilities, with certainly the most important of these being those of the benevolent committee. As with most wars, once they are over the returning soldiers flood the labour market at the same time as governments are trying to curb spending. The inevitable result is many men out of work and those in employment maybe having to take wage cuts. Blagdon, as was pointed out in some of the minuted comments, was lucky in its position and circumstances to miss many of these hardships.

Nevertheless there was some hardship and the members of the benevolent committee made great effort to help individuals and their dependents over difficult periods. From time to time claims were passed to county and area relief committees and occasionally to headquarters itself. Less serious situations could be resolved at local level by the issue of tokens which could be exchanged for food and other items in local shops. Also, in these circumstances benefit could be much more of a personal nature with cigarettes and tobacco, and in one instance Burgundy, being provided for sick members. Assistance with funeral expenses, dental treatment, and costs incurred in visiting sick relatives, indeed all the difficulties encountered where support was required, were dealt with in a sensitive and positive way.

The Secretary's address summing up the activities in September 1934 stated, '*Your Benevolent Committee have been fairly busy during the year which has just passed. A total of 13 cases have been dealt with involving a total sum of £32 2s 7d. Of this total £8 4s 7d came out of your own Branch funds. In addition to the first figure given there are other benefits which do not show in our accounts, but which have been directly conferred on the recipient through the instrumentality of the Branch. Two of the cases dealt with have entailed considerable correspondence*'.

On several occasions the minutes note money being given to 'way-farers.' Ex-servicemen travelling through the village, one presumes on foot, obviously sought out a committee member and asked for help.

In the spring of 1934 the Secretary reported that he had assisted a G. White of the Royal Fusiliers, who was on the road and in need of a meal, to the extent of 3/- (15p). This action was fully endorsed by the members. Such spontaneous funding was

Figure 3 - Memorial Chapel St Andrew's Church, Blagdon

to occur again on several occasions. In June 1936 the Secretary again reported that two distressed members (Mr W.B. James of Crumlin, once Secretary of that branch, and Mr A. Evans of Newbridge) had called on him for help. He arranged for bed and breakfast and gave them 1/- (5p) each to help them on their way.

The incident with members from South Wales came at a time when the Blagdon branch linked itself briefly with a newly formed Aberaman association. For some time there had been talk of assisting members in distressed areas. It was noticed in one of the Legion circulars that one South Wales branch could not afford a standard. The Blagdon members wanted to send 7/6d towards the cost but the President Lady Wills, '*interposed saying she would be willing to give the Standard (but wished to remain anonymous)*'. In due course, in December 1935, Messrs Teversham, Saint and Payne went to Aberaman to present the standard.

Matters did not end here, as an invitation was apparently made to the members of the South Wales branch to visit Blagdon. I say 'apparently' as no authority had been given to anyone to tender such an invitation. Nevertheless the Blagdon committee decided to overlook any misunderstanding and honour any commitment made.

So in August of the following year (1936), 23 members of the Aberaman branch travelled to Weston-super-Mare. From here the costs of transport plus entertainment at Blagdon were borne by their hosts. As records indicate,

'Our President gave them a right hearty welcome at Coombe Lodge, and threw the gardens open to them, and a most enjoyable morning was spent by all who had the privilege to be there. After an excellent dinner at the Club, the party went to the Church where they laid a wreath in the Memorial Chapel' (Fig. 3).

The rest of the afternoon was spent playing skittles and billiards, followed by tea. Much work was done by the wives of the committee men, though records also thank the contribution of Mr Cole, who kindly loaned everything required for laying the tables, Mr Dowson for the smokes, and the Oakhill Brewery Company, who donated the liquid refreshment. Later in the same year, at Christmas, the ladies of Burrington Women's Institute sent 150 filled stockings to '*our comrades at Aberaman, for distribution to the kiddies*'.

Sometimes national disasters moved members to donate some of the funds. Efford Colony[5] brought the response of one guinea in January 1932. The Gresford Colliery disaster of 1934, in which over 100 ex-servicemen lost their lives, prompted another donation, as did the East Coast floods of 1947.

Such contributions demanded that the finances of the branch be in a healthy condition, and here the work of the entertainments committee was of great importance for, apart from the pleasure afforded, funds were raised to respond to these appeals. From the start members fully supported the events organised. The most popular were whist drives and dances. Sometimes these were arranged in a series with cumulating prizes and a dance acting as a finale. Those responsible worked hard to book venues, obtain prizes, print posters and tickets, provide refreshments, and then officiate.

This was the era of the dance band, and many opinions seem to have been offered as to the merits of 'The Imperial Dance Band', or 'The Revellers', 'The Calton', 'The Scala', or later on 'The Emerald Band'.

Certainly a good time seems to have been had by all, and at many a monthly meeting the resulting accounts were presented, followed by debate as to where the profit should go. For example, the Easter Monday dance of 1934, where admission was 2/- (20p) including refreshments organized by Miss Wood, made a profit of £13 4s 9d. After some proposals and amendments it was decided that £10 was to be paid into the benevolent fund and the balance to general branch funds.

In order to diversify the range of fund raising there was in 1935 a balloon race involvement with the annual flower show. This proved quite popular and a modest profit was made. A month or so later a letter from general headquarters informed the committee that the Whitchurch branch had in fact sent their winning balloon to Spain. How the awarding of prizes was sorted out after this is not noted!

Of all activities it was long alley skittles which became very popular. In December 1933 Mr H. Shipsey was asked by the members to pick and captain a side to enter a knockout competition. In October of the following year a league was formed and the Blagdon branch entered a team, with 'Bert' Shipsey as captain and Messrs Stokes and Headford elected as selectors. For many years Bert led the side, and in later times others took over this mantle, such as Perce Fear, George Taylor, Dick Rowe and Sam Frappell. One long-standing feature of the team (and this continued well after World War II) was the opening 'set'– Ben Lyon, George Sherbourne, Reg Baber and Frank Davis, all veterans of the previous conflict. This year (2005) the team is back in action after several years of disbandment, playing regularly at the Village Club.

In the spring of 1934 the Secretary received a letter from Salanson's[6] offering, through the generosity of the Wills family, to screen to the members a free talking picture show. This was accepted, and proved so popular that the committee decided to hire some films for themselves to show in the village. On November 17th 1935 there was a talking picture programme given in the Parish Room by Salanson's. The charge to the committee was £5 10s for an afternoon and evening performance. Admission prices were to be:

Afternoon	Children under 12	3d & 4d
	Adults	9d & 1/-
Evening		9d & 1/-

Perhaps these were the first public showing of talking pictures in the village.

Nationally, the mid-1930s was a time of celebration and consternation. 1935 saw the Silver Jubilee of George V, and in 1937 the Coronation of his son George VI. Intervening was the abdication crisis of Edward VIII. With the jubilee the Legion played its part by entering the fancy dress competition in the Blagdon festivities. The same was done two years later with the coronation. The indefatigable Miss Wood and her helpers sold coronation emblems and raised a considerable sum. As part of the national celebrations, on June 27th 1937 there was a parade in Hyde Park of ex-servicemen. Twelve members, together with the standard, made the journey. Later these individuals were each to receive a letter of commemoration concerning the event.

As the decade begins to fade it is interesting to note the names and responsibilities of the officers. This résumé of the **1937 AGM** can provide some of this. The following were elected (in fact re-elected):

President	Lady Wills
Vice-President	Mr H.J. Frise
Chairman	Rev. Marriott
Secretary	Capt. Teversham
Treasurer	Mr Headford
Standard Bearer	Mr Saint
Auditors	Mr Frise & Mr Harrison

Other committee members (who retired after one year)
Messrs Fraser, Cryer, F. Light and Ash

Remembrance Sunday

It was decided that this year it would be November 14th (as yet there seemed to be no national date set.) Morning Service was to be held in the Baptist Chapel. £1 was to be spent on a wreath. Mr Shipsey and Mr Cryer to be bearers and a bugler was to be in attendance. Capt. Teversham was to be OC parade.

Distressed Areas

As the situation was not so acute it was decided not to send a donation as yet.

Poppy Day

Miss Wood and her helpers had arrangements well in hand.

Other business

Mr Shipsey raised the question of the amount that the skittles team was being asked to pay for the use of the Village Club alley. A letter was to be sent asking the Village Club to reconsider the amount demanded.

Vote of thanks

Mr H.J. Frise proposed a vote of thanks to the chairman.

Signed   N. Jean Wills
October 17th 1938

It should be added that these officers remained with their responsibilities until after the war, the exception being Capt. Teversham, who rejoined the forces. Mr Headford as was mentioned earlier, became Secretary and Treasurer.

On Whit Monday 1939 the Legion organised and held a fête. After considerable preparation and effort the event was held with a healthy profit of over £17 being made, which was duly credited to branch funds. Lessons were learnt from running this first (and, as records go, last) fête. Letters of thanks were sent to Messrs Godwin, Dowson, Redwood, Nelson, Goodman and Capt. Harris for their assistance. It was to be the last celebration to take place before the outbreak of World War II a few months later. This west country 'World of Mrs Miniver'[7] was about to change and, with several aspects of village life, to change forever.

After the declaration of war took place on 3rd September 1939, the first meeting was held in the George Inn. The change of location was probably because the Village Club was in use as an A.R.P. (air raid precautions) headquarters. The entertainment programme was to be modified to accommodate any last minute changes. Parcels were to be sent to servicemen, some already overseas. A note at the bottom of the minutes gives these members as:

R. Harvey	Don Clarke	Ken Collier	C. Duval
F. Walters	Horace Brown	Don Williams	
S. Croker	W. Glanville	Ken Best	

A meeting in November decided to send 5/- (25p) postal orders and a suitable letter to the five serving men (K. Best, H. Brown, D. Clark, W. Glanville, and S. Croker) as a first effort. The meeting also learned, an hour or so before, that the 10pm curfew regarding charitable establishments had been lifted. So arrangements for the Christmas whist drive and dance in the New Year could go ahead. It was decided, however, not to hold the annual dinner.

In January 1940 the first foods in Britain were rationed: butter 4oz per week, bacon and ham 4oz, and sugar 12oz. Two months later it was the turn of meat, then margarine and cooking fats. Whether it was as a result of these restrictions or not, an entry made during the February meeting, noting that several members were ill, makes interesting reading (and here I hope that the families of those concerned are not offended.)

'It was proposed by Mr Headford and seconded by Mr Hollier that Messrs H. Young and F. Monk call upon Messrs R. Baber and M. Fraser, who are ill, and to obtain any nourishing food they require up to the value of 5/-'. Apparently there were regulations regarding restaurants, where the maximum which could be charged for a meal was 5/- (25p), and perhaps this generosity was meant to keep in line with these new rules.

Also, the introduction of rationing had an influence on the running of dances and the food which could be provided. In March of that year it was decided that the entrance charge should be reduced to 1/6d (7½p) and refreshments, *'to run at popular prices'*.

In February of 1940 there appears a strange note of discord: an Extraordinary Meeting had been called. The only reference to it was in the AGM later in the year where it was decided that the minutes of this meeting, *'should not be read but preserved and when the matter had been disposed of burned'*.

In April the Secretary, Mr Teversham, resigned, now being a member of H.M. Forces. Before this, and whilst being an officer of the branch, he had served in Palestine with the League Plebiscite Police in 1938. Now in 1940 he was again in uniform.

In the AGM of 1940 Mr Headford stated that, *'The year had been very ordinary in spite of the war'*. Messrs Teversham, Young, Collier and Harvey had joined the Services. Other members had joined the Home Guard, ARP, and first aid services. This meant, obviously, that attendance at branch meetings was going to be lower, and in fact some of them were cancelled through lack of numbers.

Poppy Day collections went on as usual. The December 1940 issue of the parish magazine records, *'that a record sum was raised in response to our appeal. Our thanks are due to Miss Wood and her fellow collectors for their efforts and to all who gave on behalf of a cause which has more than ever a claim upon our sympathy and help'*.

	£	s	d
Mrs Teversham	4	4	9
Mrs T. Saint	2	14	11
Mrs B. Young	3	5	10
Mrs C. Davis	5	18	7
Mrs V. Ash	2	2	4
Mrs B. King	6	6	1
Miss D. Wood	3	0	1
Mrs F. Cryer (Depot)		6	6
Miss B. Small (C'House)	3	2	3
The Battery office		6	8
Mrs Frise		9	8
Subtotal	31	17	1
The Parish Church	6	6	8
St Hugh's Church		5	0
The Methodist Chapel	1	6	6
Legion wreath & other sales	2	0	0
Subtotal	9	18	2
Total	41	15	3

The 'Depot' is thought to be Mrs Cryer's house (Sovereign Cottage) in the High Street, a central position ideally situated for the storing of collection boxes. The 'Battery office' is a little more interesting. In the latter part of 1940 it seems certain that Blagdon played host to a Northumberland Hussars yeomanry regiment. These men then became part of the 102 Royal Artillery (B Battery). A regimental photograph has come to light which was taken, it appears, though there is no absolute verification, in the Court grounds, prior to posting to North Africa. The Poppy Day collection may have caught the unit as it was leaving the area. The same December magazine from which the collection figures have been taken contains a cryptic message from, one presumes, the Rev. Marriott. The article thanked the 60 ladies who gave of their time to provide meals and went on to note '… *that during the first three months of its existence the Canteen provided just under 2,000 hot meals, nearly 400 cold suppers, and served, amongst lesser refreshments, some 5,000 cups of tea and coffee'* for the soldiers (although this last word is not mentioned). The author stressed the *'friendship made between ourselves and the men from the north'*.[8] Great care was being taken in these post-Dunkirk times that censorship regulations were not violated. No names were given, even that of the letter-writer appearing as a line of asterisks.

The AGMs held in October or November of each year were the ideal times for deciding upon the Christmas gifts for serving members. Those overseas received a little more than those at home, and here, to solve one problem, Ireland and the Shetland Isles were defined as 'abroad'. In January 1941, 44 postal orders had been sent to the serving men and the one serving woman. By March 1945, 99 members had received gifts − 42 at 10/- (50p) and 57 at 7/6 (37½p), giving an expenditure of just over £44.

To obtain such funds, whist drives and dances continued as in pre-war days though with the restrictions on victuals and fuel. What also helped were the nationally organised campaigns such as 'Salute the Soldier' and 'Warship Week'.

As the end of the war drew near there were discussions as to whether the money should be sent to the serving men or transferred to a Welcome Home Fund for gifts and celebration when they returned. At the branch meeting of January 1946 members firmly voted for such funds to go to the latter.

The records of the 'Blagdon Boys and Girls Welcome Home and Comforts Fund' still exist. The accounts were audited by Mr Headford, with Mrs E.R. Skillman being Honorary Organising Secretary and Rev. E. Marriott the Chairman. Income and expenditure from 1941 to 1946 is there in all its detail.

The main event, **The Reunion Supper**, is believed to have been held in December 1946 in the Parish Room (Fig. 4). In all 93 names are listed as normally living in Blagdon and therefore should *'have consideration when [the] distribution fund commence[s]'*. Mrs Florrie Addicott, who attended the occasion, said for her the highlight was a fine speech made by Miss Gwynville Lawson (née Day).

FIRST RE-UNION SUPPER FOR BLAGDON EX-SERVICEMEN was held at Blagdon Parish Hall last night. The supper was organised by Mrs. E. R. Skillman from funds raised in the village by her band of helpers, who are seen standing behind the table on the left.

Figure 4 - 'Welcome Home' Re-union Supper

Sadly, five names appear as making the supreme sacrifice — Sir Peter Wills, Harry Lye, Walter Pole, Brian Dufty and Joseph Wagstaff. It is curious that the others who died in service — Kenneth Cole, Edward Gracie and Edmond Vigor — are not mentioned.

Sir Peter Wills was killed in Italy in the closing phase of the war, in April 1945. Only a year or so earlier, in February 1943, Lady Wills had sent a letter to the Blagdon British Legion thanking them for the message of congratulation sent to Sir Peter on the occasion of reaching his majority. At the November AGM two years later she was to read a letter of appreciation from a colleague of her son who was with him prior to his death. The anniversary trees in The Coombe (Fig. 5) were now of sombre significance. [9]

Figure 5 - The anniversary trees in Blagdon Coombe
celebrating the 21 birthdays of Sir Peter Wills

As the celebrations were overtaken by resolution for the future it was time to close the accounts regarding the festivities. However the fund was found to be in the red — not dramatically so, but enough to warrant one more money-raising effort. This resulted in the horse show and gymkhana held in The Coombe. This event was to gain a momentum all of its own, and to become one of the prime dates in the Blagdon calendar for some years to come. Apart from paying off the small debt regarding the welcome home fund, monies raised were given to the Red Cross.

The returning men and women now swelled the ranks of the Legion. In the local branch women were not admitted, though there was talk of such things, but they could be made honorary members. Times were nevertheless changing. Rembrance Day was now fixed, the first record of this being in the 1946 observance.

Benevolence work continued and here the usual cigarettes and tobacco were bought for sick members. On one occasion Mr G. Addicott received some malt oil whilst ill and conveyed his appreciation to the committee.

In a more serious vein two protracted pension claims were supported and pursued by the Branch. One concerned J. Jeffries of Nempnett, where leave to appeal to the House of Lords was turned down. The other concerned Charles Westbrook, son of the old headmaster.

The **AGM of 1948** marks a change in the Blagdon British Legion. Members who had been active during the war were now joined by those leaving the services. Of the founders, Dr Pineo and Mr S.G. Starr had passed away, Rev. Marriott was unwell, and Mr Headford looking to lessen his burden.

Attending the meeting on November 1st 1948 at the Village Club were The Lady President, Lady Wills, C.F. Payne, H.R. Headford, W.M. Andres, V. Ash, R.A. Baber, L.W. Barnes, D. Bray, A.H.G. Campbell, C.A. Cole, K.Collier, F. Davies, W.D. Drake, A.E. Filer, G. Filer, M. Fraser, A. Green, F.W.D. Grayson, *L.*(?) Hall, W.J. Harrison, G. *Hogg* (?), F.H. Hollier, J.W. Hope, R.B. Jones, F.H. Light, B. Lyons, W.H. Lyons, K.G. Nelson, R. *Ryley*(?), E. Saint, T.E. Saint, G. Sherborne, H.M. Sweeting, R.J. Vowles, N. Wilson, K.L.Yorath, N.M. Fisher, R.S. Winter, B.E. Tucker, G.P. Hider, C.E. Lyons, R.S. Crockett, G.E. Taylor, L.J. Tidcombe, R.P. Gibb, C. Price, W.J. Colborne, R.H. Headford, and H. Salway.

Apologies: Apologies for absence were received through the President from the Chairman and Mrs Richard Hill.

Minutes: Of the AGM held on 19th October 1947 were approved.

Secretary's report.
1. Loss of Vice-President Mr T. Frise.
2. Hope that the Chairman, The Reverend E. Marriott, would be soon be fully recovered.
3. Some subscriptions for the year ending 30th September 1948 had not been paid.
4. He hoped that the poor attendances at the monthly meetings would improve.

Finances: Balances stood as follows:

General	£18	8s	1d
Benevolent	£104	5s	3d
Entertainment	£108	13s	10d

Election of officers: The following were elected to stand for the coming year:

President	Lady Wills
Vice-President	Preb. E. Marriott
Chairman	R.P.D. Gibb
Vice-Chairman	A.G.H. Campbell
Treasurer	H.R. Headford
Secretary	N.M Fisher

The following new members were elected to sit on committee:

	Retiring members
L.W. Barnes	K. Collier
C.A. Cole	G. Grayson
R.J. Vowles	A. Harris
R.S. Winter	G. Filer

Poppy Day Organiser: Miss D. M. Wood

Standard Bearer: Mr T.E. Saint

Deputy Standard Bearer: Mr M. Fraser

Entertainments and Service Committees: to be elected at the next General Committee meeting.

Dance: Mr T. Saint reported that an Old Time Dance had been arranged for December 3rd. A piano was to be hired for the occasion.

Whist Drive: This was arranged for 4th December. The President offered turkey, whisky and (other) prizes.

Dinner: To take place in early February; a summer outing was also suggested.

County Subscription: £2 2s was agreed for the forthcoming year.

The meeting was closed.   *N. J. Wills   November 7th 1949*

In these early post-war years, and to a certain extent before, there were circulars distributed and much discussion at all levels in the British Legion about such topics as clothing for those leaving the forces, loans to establish small businesses, and above all, the need for more housing. Concerning this last point many married couples in the neighbourhood were in shared accommodation, sometimes in the most difficult of circumstances, and with the birth rate expected to rise conditions were not going to improve.

The local authority (Axbridge RDC) seems to have acted rather tardily in this respect, with little in the shape of plans for building new houses in Blagdon – indeed up to 1947 only six units were envisaged. The depth of feeling over this situation can be judged by a branch meeting held on 12th May 1947, when no fewer than 72 members attended to hear of the latest housing developments.

Mr B.J. Gallop, Chairman of Blagdon Parish Council, was present, and also Messrs Godwin and Downey, who were local Rural District councillors. These officers had been asked to explain the situation, and were told in no uncertain terms that the plan (for six houses) was totally unsatisfactory. Could it be that such pressure resulted in the dramatic change of policy? For within a few years Westcroft (1947/48), Boyd's Orchard, now Garston Cottages, (1948/49), and then Eastcroft (1949/52) were built – forty dwellings in total.

The late 1940s heralded the start of the children's Christmas parties organised by the British Legion. In the latter part of 1948, Mr Marsh (a non-member) informed the committee that there was the possibility of a grant from the NFS[10] to help towards the costs of such an event. Arrangements went ahead and on January 8th 1949 the first of these took place, cost £15 5s 7d. Personally, I can certainly remember looking forward to these, and with the date usually in January or February it seemed to make the festive season last that little bit longer.

With a programme of refreshments, films, and games, these parties were held every year until 1955. In the penultimate year 163 children attended with the cost being about £22 plus £6 for films. The minutes record thanks to Mr Stevens for the milk and Mrs Tucker and helpers for the refreshments. Early in 1956 it was decided not to go ahead that year as funds were not sufficient and this marked the end, as the parties were never restarted.

As the new decade of the 1950s dawned, the Legion was in a strong overall position. Unfortunately it was to experience two tragedies. On August 23rd 1950 Mr A.J. Greenslade was killed in a motor accident at Redhill. 'Jim' had been an active member since the war years and in 1949 had succeeded Mr Headford as Treasurer.

His long service career with the Royal Navy included several years on the battleship 'George V' and the ill-fated 'Hood'. He was the popular licensee of the Queen Adelaide, having taken over from Archie Harris, the previous tenant, in somewhat acrimonious circumstances. At his funeral the list of mourners is a veritable 'Who's Who' in Blagdon at the time, with every organisation wishing to be represented.

The second tragedy took place two years later. Here, in the minutes of the April 1952 meeting there is the chilling record that, *'The meeting then broke up at the request of the Chairman of the Parish Council Mr Gallop, that as many members as possible would help in the search for Mr Nelson.'*

Ken Nelson was an honorary member of the branch and had been active since before the war. He had never held office but is mentioned on many occasions helping with the various events — indeed in the current year he was one of those appointed to visit sick members. The search was successful, if you can use that word. Ken Nelson had taken his own life. Bluebell Wood in the top part of the Coombe was not a pleasant place to be that day.

As the 1950s progressed those officials who had steered the association for many years stepped back. Lady Wills retired as President in 1954, although later she was to be Vice-President for a number of years. Sir John, her son, was also a Vice-President, starting in the same year and continuing until the very end. The Reverend, now Prebendary, Marriott, a founder member, became President and in 1955 was given a Certificate of Merit from the movement. Two years later a certificate was awarded to Mr Headford for his sterling services. The honorary woman of the era, Miss Daisy Wood, had already retired in 1950.

The mid-1950s also saw a change of rector. The Reverent Edwin Neep soon made his presence felt by changing the Remembrance Day pattern. He insisted upon the now normal observance of the two-minutes silence followed by a service at the church. In 1958 the Legion was invited to attend Church to participate. As the Blagdon branch had kept to its routine since the early 1930s there was much consternation. Minutes state that, *'It appears that whatsoever the outcome the Rector will still hold the Service at the appropriate time whether the Legion attends or no'*. Perhaps it is no coincidence that his predecessor at St Andrew's had now left and a new system could be introduced without any embarrassment. At the next AGM when the matter was brought up for discussion the change was agreed to. In 1959 both chapels attended, making this an annual event, there now not being any service outside St Andrew's.

Whilst still on the subject of remembrance and parades, the branch was honoured in 1954 by the standard bearer, Mr M. Fraser, representing the branch at the Royal

Fig. 6 - The First World War (1914–1918) plaque
Memorial Chapel St Andrew's Church, Blagdon.

To commemorate "INHABITANTS OF THIS VILLAGE FORMER SCHOLARS AT
BLAGDON AND CHARTERHOUSE SCHOOLS WORSHIPPERS IN THE
CHURCHES OF ST ANDREW AND ST HUGH OR THEIR SONS".

Festival of Remembrance at the Albert Hall. During the televised broadcast Murdo was one of those bearers selected for close-up individual shots, appreciated by all those in Blagdon who had televisions at the time.

A meeting of the branch on May 7th 1956 expressed the desire to support the need of a '*Memorial for Blagdon & District and those who fell and served in the last War*'. Already in the memorial chapel (Fig. 3) there were wooden furnishings, a memorial tablet and a book of remembrance for those who served and fell in the previous World War. It was decided to add a candelabra with six lamps and another inscribed tablet to the fallen (Fig. 7). Also, all those who served in the 1939/45 conflict would have their names added to the book of remembrance (Fig. 8). At a service held on March 20th 1957 this new war memorial was dedicated.

Fig. 7 - The Second World War (1939–1945) plaque

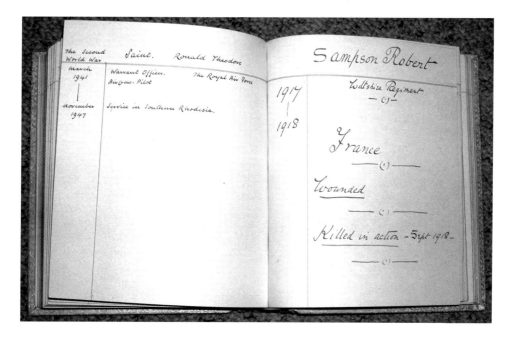

Fig. 8 - Book of Remembrance

Memorial Chapel, St Andrew's Church, Blagdon

In the post-war period there started a link with the British Limbless Ex-Servicemen's Association, BLESMA, (Bristol), part of the Legion. The first mention of this is in the minutes of the 1949 AGM. BLESMA had two members in the Blagdon branch, A.H.G. Campbell and K. Cook. For many years social events were organised, with the local members being entertained at various venues in Bristol and, of course, their hosts being invited to reciprocal arrangements in Blagdon. A summer skittles competition was started at the Village Club to raise funds for the BLESMA association. This competition is still in being, though not by name, and monies raised now go to local charities.

The initial enthusiasm when the skittles team was formed, with Bert Shipsey as captain, continued for a long time. Minutes over the years talk of the rising cost of transport and how much subsidy should come from various funds and the number of honorary members permissible. In 1965, when the Club became licensed, the question of the need to pay an annual membership was discussed. In the beginning the Legion paid the subscriptions for the players, though over the next year or so individuals paid for themselves. Later in its existence the team was to lose much of its identity with the Legion due to changing social circumstances.

As the AGM of 1948 saw a considerable change in officers, so the pattern set in the 1950s was also of importance. The majority of these elected members were to see the Legion through to its closure in 1979.

Essentially these officers were, from 1958 onwards:

President: W.R.T. Young (1958-1979)
Vice-Presidents: Jean, Lady Wills (1958-1960), Sir John Wills (1958- 1979), Preb. Marriott (1958-1966), Mr Birch (1961-1979), Mr Reeves (1961-1967)
Chairman: R.P. Gibb
Vice-Chairman: Col. Yorath (1958-1965), K. Cook (1966-1979)
Treasurer: Mr Read (1958-1977), Mr Leach (1978-1979)
Secretary: Mr Barnes (1958-1969 & 1977-1978), Mr Fear (1970-1976)
Service Secretary: Mr Barnes (1970-1978)

From the early 1960s there were signs that the Blagdon branch was, in many respects, struggling to survive. At the April 4th meeting in 1960 Col. Yorath wished it to be recorded '*That some concern was being felt by the poor attendance at Branch Meetings*'. In July of the same year there was the laying-up of the Sandford standard. The omens were not good. The traditional pattern of whist drives and dances had had their day. The annual whist drive prior to Christmas was discontinued in 1970 as returns were getting lower and lower. Local dances became area dances before they, too, disappeared from the year's programme.

So the two main forms of income disappeared. Yet in the early 1960s Mr Birch, a new vice-president, explored the possibility of opening the gardens of many of the residents of Church Street to the public, at a price of course! This went ahead and was a great success, and so for many years (except after the bitter winter of 1962/63) and really right up to the demise of the Legion it was an annual event. The church was decorated by the Chew Valley Floral Society, thus augmenting the attraction.

Proceeds went to the Commonwealth Fund for the Blind but the Blagdon Legion who organized the event retained a percentage of the takings. In 1964 the sum made was £51 15s 6d, from which 10% was given to branch benevolent funds. By 1967 receipts had risen to £320. Occasionally the Legion gave its 'cut' to local causes like the school swimming pool. A comment by the Treasurer at the 1964 AGM states that '*A cheque from the Horse Show and the percentage from the Open Gardens kept funds in the clear*'. The actual contribution from the former was no doubt welcome, but it is difficult to define from the records what the amount was and how many there were.

By the end of the 1960s it was obvious that the branch was in difficulties. Although theoretically having quite a number on roll, the individuals who attended meetings and sought responsibility became fewer and fewer. Changes in the headquarters did not help. After using the Village Club since 1930, the Legion found that it was unable to book a room for its monthly meetings. The steward, Henry Buxton, was approached in an attempt to sort out the matter, but to no avail. So at the AGM of 1957 it was decided to move to the George Inn. This unfortunately proved temporary, as in the spring of the following year (1958) this pub closed its doors for the last time.

So another move was made, this time to the Seymour Arms. But by the early 1970s meetings were once again held at the original venue.

It was in the 1970s that the decline of the branch became terminal. Virtually all of the founder members had passed away and those now holding office had done so for many years. Whist drives and dances were no more, annual dinners became suppers before they, too, were not held at all. In 1977 the entertainment and benevolent accounts were closed. There was still a membership of 55, but few of these attended meetings. The spirit of the 1930s, where enthusiasm bounded from every page of the minutes, was no longer there. The March meeting of 1979 was cancelled, as were the ones in April and May. June attracted four members, with September and October not doing any better. So really by the time of the AGM (3rd December 1979) the future, or lack of it, was no longer in doubt.

The following members were present:

Mr R. T. Young
Mr R. P. D. Gibb
Mr K. Cook
Mr R. Baber
Mr M. Fraser
Mr R. E. Leach
Mr L. G. Carroll

They requested the Secretary to approach headquarters with a view to winding up the Branch but retaining the Armistice Day parade, the British Legion standard, and the Poppy Day organisation.

This was to be the last meeting – the Blagdon branch of the Royal British Legion was no more.[11] Two names on this valedictory roll appeared in the very first meetings back in 1930: Murdo Fraser and Reg Baber, both stalwart members who gave of their time for so many years. I wonder what their thoughts were that evening when memories of almost fifty years of service were consigned to history.

1   Some, such as Mr A. Chamberlain, chose to remain at Churchill.

2   Rector of Blagdon, 1929-1958

3   Proposed and passed *that filing past the memorial and reading of the names of the fallen be disposed with*, meeting of October 3rd 1931. Certainly in modern times the latter takes place.

4   Headmaster of Blagdon Primary School (April 1933 – April 1952)

5   A tuberculosis hospital run by the Devon and Cornwall Ex-Servicemen's Association, situated near Plymouth, closed some years ago.

6   A large photography company in Bristol.

7   The 1942 film, Mrs Miniver. The story of a wartime family, starring Walter Pidgeon and Greer Garson, which did much to raise morale when spirits were at a low ebb.

8   The same December magazine also includes a letter from the Regiment's Commanding Officer, again not signed.

9   A row of trees planted in a 'half-moon' field near the wood, one for each childhood birthday up to 21.

10   National Fire Service.

11   'Royal' since 1971.

References and acknowledgements

Minute books of the Blagdon Branch of the British Legion, committee meetings 1930-1979.
St Andrew's, Blagdon, and St Hugh's, Charterhouse-on-Mendip, parish magazine (Issues for January 1931 and December 1940.)
John and Sybil Gallop.
Iris Veater.
Sam Frappell.
Les Barnes (as mentioned.)

A complete chronological list of British Legion officials is available in the BLHS archives.

FLO ADDICOTT
1912–2003

Tony Staveacre

'One of my brothers was killed by a horse before I was born. He was only a little boy, on his way to school. They used to play in the fields along Dipland, in Powell's farm. The schoolchildren used to go out in those two fields there and play. And there was a horse out there and my brother got kicked to death by it when he was only four years old. I think the kids were teasing the horse, and it kicked out, and my brother happened to be the unlucky one.

We were a family of thirteen. My father was a Devon man. He walked from Devon to Butcombe when they were starting to work on the lake. He had heard that there would be labouring jobs there, so he walked all the way from Devon to here. And he lodged with my grandmother. Green Lane Cottage it used to be called. They took in lodgers there, my grandfather and grandmother, about ten lodgers at a time. From what I can gather, there was a cooked meal there one night and the pudding was apple dumplings, and my father took a real fancy to the apple dumplings, which my mother had made, she being the daughter of the house. So that's how they met, through the apple dumplings! That's how that turned out. They were married quite soon after they met. Her maiden name was Dear. I never met my father's parents. But I did meet his brothers and sisters. He was the only one of that family to get married, my father. There were two sisters and another brother. The brother was a fisherman but the girls, they never done anything at all.

My parents, they had eleven children. Quite a family! And I was the baby. Harry, Robert, Edith, Anna, Jack, Albert, Cecil, Lloyd and Florence. And there were two still-born children. We slept head to toe in the bed. There were only three bedrooms, so with a family like that you can imagine it was quite a crush. Grove Cottage on the Bath Road.

My brother, Sammy (Cecil), was a gardener, down at Bourne, up until my father died. Then he stayed at home and ran the newspaper business. Albert was more or less a farm worker. He worked for the Wills estate, and he worked out at Dipland farm. He married the daughter out there. Jack was an ordinary labourer, he did work for anybody any time. Lloyd worked for Cecil Payne, used to drive the lorry. Everyone called him Toot, I don't know why. And my sisters all went into service in Bristol.

My mother used to go out chimney-sweeping, to get a bit of money in! I used to go beside of her. And there were certain places I specially liked going to because I used to get a piece of cake in those people's houses, and I thought that was wonderful! And father used to cut hair and shave people from his bedside. They used to kneel down beside the bed and cut their hair. My mother would lather their faces, and father would shave them. He was paralysed, you see, after an accident. I never ever saw him walk. He fell down some steps at the pub – the Seymour Arms. He injured his back, and never walked again. He was in the hospital for seventeen weeks, they couldn't do anything for him. Of course I was only a little girl at the time. From then on, he never walked. But he carried on with his newspaper business. He'd have the papers on his bed, and sort them all out for the customers.

I went to school in Blagdon every day. There was an infant class in the bottom room: that was Standard One and Two. And then in the big room, which was all one big room together, there was Standard Three and Four and Five and Six and Seven. There were three teachers and one headmaster in them days. I can remember Miss Bath, Miss Pryor and Miss Puddy. And the head-master was Chummy Westbrook. They were very strict. We used to do cooking, the girls, and the boys would do gardening. They had a school garden over where the old people's bungalows are now. And we used to do our cooking in the Parish Room in them days. And the teacher for that would come up from Wedmore but I forget her name. We used to have a sewing lesson, and we children would make our own clothes when we were at school. We didn't have a uniform, we girls wore ordinary dresses with pinafores. Seems funny, doesn't it, now?

And when I come home from school, off would come my shoes! And if I wanted to play I'd have to play in bare feet. Wasn't allowed to wear my shoes 'cos we couldn't afford to buy new ones, so that was that. We didn't have time to play a lot, but two or three of the King girls, and the Lyons's from Sladacre Lane, used to come as far as my house, and we used to play outside my house. We would play 'Lamp Out', which was where you'd have four corners and one would stand in each corner and there'd be another in the middle. And when we did say 'Lamp Out', the one in the middle had to catch one of the ones in the corners. And then whoever she did catch, she had to go in the middle. We used to play with hoops, we could take our hoops to school. And spinning tops. I don't suppose you can buy a spinning top today.

Sometimes we used to go down to the station to play with a milk truck. There was a milk trolley down there, which the farmers used to put their milk in, and we'd climb on to this milk truck, and somebody would push us along the platform there. Sometimes the blooming old truck would go down on to the railway lines and 'twas a real scrabble then to get it back up before the train came in! That's the sort of fun we used to have in them days.

And you know where the tennis courts are now, just opposite where Grove Cottage is, well there used to be a ditch down after side there in the road. And we used to call that the Sand Hole, where it went through into the tennis court. Sand from the road dust used to collect there, so we would go up there and play in the sand, make sand-castles. That was our beach! And we would play tennis in the road! Copying the tennisers. We would put a piece of string across the road, from the wall to the hedge, we had wooden bats, and we would pinch a tennis ball from the long grass, where the tennisers had lost them. Of course every time a car came we had to unhitch this piece of rope and let it go down on the ground for them to go by. But there weren't many cars in them days. Very few. The baker had two horses, a pony and a horse. They had a van to deliver the bread, and the pony, Topsy – the young boy would take that out with deliveries later on.

My mother used to make pots of tea for the tennisers. And they would bring their own sandwiches. Only a few select people would play tennis. Ted Filer – he's dead now. And Miss Wood. And the Miss Bakers and Chum Ash. And Reg Wigley the butcher. And Mr Ladbrooke from Ubley and the girl Ladbrookes would come over to Blagdon to play tennis. It wasn't a club, but you had to pay so much per season if you wanted to play.

The first wireless programme I ever heard was on earphones up at Swiss Cottage, where Frederick Wood used to live. The solicitor, down Wrington. Miss Wood had this wireless and when I went up there with the papers one day, Miss Wood came to the door and she said to me 'Would you like to hear this wireless?' and I said 'Nooo!'

I wondered what it was. 'Oh,' she said, 'you come in a minute and do listen.' So I did, and she put these ear-phones on me and she said 'That's coming all the way from Cardiff!' I just couldn't believe it. I heard this music coming through those headphones. It was amazing. That's when I first heard the wireless. Of course, we had the films in the village: Hughie Martin, he had a film projector, of some sort, and he used to set it up in the Parish Room and we would pay tuppence to go and see these pictures – and they be all upside down, and he'd say 'Oh, wait a minute, I've got them all muddled up!' – 'twas a proper shambles really, but we did use to enjoy these pictures.

Once a year we had a Sunday school outing down Weston. We went in a charabanc. Twister Lyons' charabanc. Mr Lambrick, the rector, he always went with us. And if it was a wet day, he would treat us all to the pictures for an hour. The vicar was very well liked in those days. He used to keep a pet crow over home. And this crow would go around with him all over the place. On his shoulder. If you look in the church, in the window on the left aisle up at the top, there's a picture and there's a crow, in the dots at the end of the writing. That's the crow, in Mr Lambrick's window.

I never ever went to Bristol when I was a girl. Not until after I'd lost mother and father. Because mother died when I was 15, and father died when I was 18. Mother died of yellow jaundice. I had to do all the house work after mother died. And the cooking, and the washing, and see that father was clean, you know, wash and do for him. I had really no idea how to do any cooking, so I used to go in and sit on father's bed and he'd tell me what to do. I know I had a rabbit to cook one day, and I took it in and took a bowl of water, and he made me skin this rabbit. Oh dear, I cried and I cried, but I still had to do it, he made me do it. And then I had to soak it in salt water, and then I had to cook it the next day. And I'd never done any cooking, but I did make this rabbit stew, by father telling me what to do. Turned out very good as it happened. From then on I had to do all the cooking and everything, and he did give me sixpence a week from then on. Lot of money wasn't it?

After father died, I carried on the paper business with Sammy. I had to deliver the papers in Blagdon as well. I had a bicycle, which my father had had made for me. Bert Pearce made it out of two or three old bicycles. I used it to go around Blagdon, and to deliver the papers. I used to go up Two Trees, to Parker's Farm. Then I'd go down Ellick Road, and come straight down over the hill, and straight up to Butcombe with all the papers.

I had a friend, she would come with me on the bike, she would sit on the saddle and I would stand on the pedals. And we would come whizzing down the hill, it were wonderful! People used to report me to father when he was alive, for going too fast over the hills.

The papers were only a penny each in them days. The *Weston Mercury* was tuppence. The Sunday papers, I think they were all tuppence each in them days. They didn't pay for deliveries then, but at Christmas time they would give me presents, maybe a penny or tuppence. Miss Bath who lived down the farmhouse there, who was a school teacher: she once gave me a shilling! And I thought 'Oh good gracious me!' and I said to her 'Do you want any change?' and she said 'No – that's all for you.' I thought that was wonderful.

Then I had to go round with the papers at night, when we had the evening papers. We had to go down to the station to collect those. The Pink 'Un on a Saturday night, with the football results. And Vic Carpenter and his mother, they used to deliver the Green 'Un. So they had to go down to the station also to collect theirs. And we'd come rushing up the hill, so as to sell our papers first. And we did go into the Village Club, where they would be busy playing billiards. We did creep up the stairs – we had to be ever so quiet – to sell these Pink 'Uns. We'd always sell all our papers – but poor old Vic Carpenter, he'd still be standing out there on the corner by the Seymour Arms, trying to sell his papers at ten o'clock at night. 'Twas great fun, those days were!

I was quite contented as a girl, you know. It never worried me a bit that I had all this work to do and the family to look after. I met my husband when I was delivering the papers. He lived down at Ridge End. His father was a postman. And when I had newspapers for Butcombe – if Edgar's father was on that round, he would take the papers on up for me. I can remember one day, he had an inspector visiting. So I didn't attempt to go near Mr Addicott that day because I knew he wasn't really allowed to take our papers on the post. So of course I ignored him that day and that was all right. But the first house that Mr Addicott took the post to, with the Inspector coming with him, the man came to the door and said 'Well, where's my paper gone to, then?', and that got him into trouble, didn't it?

Edgar's family lived out in the woods, up by the Ham, in the keeper's cottage out there. And his parents used to come down to the Seymour Arms every night of the week, Sundays and all, just for Mr Addicott to have his pint of beer, and Granny Addicott to have a drop of whisky. And then they'd walk all the way back up again, through the woods in the dark. Didn't matter what the weather was. I don't think I could have done a thing like that. Mr Nelson was the postmaster then, and all the postmen had to be at the post office at 6 o'clock, and they'd stand in a row for the postmaster to inspect their boots and their uniform. One morning he said to Mr Addicott, 'You haven't cleaned your boots this morning!' And Mr Addicott said: 'If you had to go up through Blagdon woods, you'd soon know why my boots are dirty!' Anyway he had to clean 'em, before he went out on his round. Different today, isn't it?

We were married in 1935, I think, at St Andrew's Church, and had the reception down at Lake View, where Edgar's mother lived in them days. Edgar was a carpenter, for Frank Puddy. Seven years he was apprenticed to him. Then he was working for Chappie Payne. He did the undertaking for him, made the coffins. And when Chappie gave up the undertaking, Edgar took that over as well. Finished up doing all the funerals then, Edgar did. He'd make the coffins here at home.

The only time I went on a train was with Edgar: we went to Blackpool to see the lights. 'Twas fixed through the paper – the *Evening Post* took a lot of groups from Blagdon. We went up Blackpool Tower. 'Twas frightening to me, really. I didn't think much of the Illuminations.

Edgar was the only one of those four brothers that got an apprenticeship. Arthur was a farm labourer, Harry was a gardener at Butcombe Rectory, and Fred was a general labourer. When we first married we lived at home, at Grove Cottage. Cecil was the only one of my brothers who was still living there then. Jack had gone, he disappeared. We never knew what had happened to him. During the Second World War he came to see me, and surprised me really – I hadn't seen him for years. He was living at Midsomer Norton then. He was in a bit of a mess. Edgar was gone in the army, so I fitted Jack up with one of Edgar's suits. And made him have a bath out in our back kitchen , 'cos we didn't have a bathroom then. I gave him a good meal. He stayed here for about three days I think. Never said a word. And then he shoved off again, and we never seen anything more of him after. But he was a bit on the queer side, you know. He was a bit lacking somewhere or other. My father was a bit on the cruel side. He didn't have much patience with Jack, and I suppose that's why he cleared off. I think my father would have been a very cruel man if he had had his health and strength. But mother was lovely person. Very tender and very loving, she was.

I've lived here in Bell Square for 65 years. Only ever lived in two houses all my life.

Of course, the village has grown a lot. I used to know where everybody lived, and their names. You had good neighbours always in them days, you didn't hear people fighting and grumbling. There was no-one jealous of one another or anything like that in them days. We were all like one family. As a girl, when I'd go up to Coombe Lodge with the papers, I used to go to the kitchen door, to see the cook, and she always had a little bag there ready for me with some cakes and that in. 'Cos we were a poor family actually, our family. I haven't had an easy life, I can tell you. But I got through it all right. The very best time in my life, really speaking, is right now. Other than my health, I got a real easy life now! Very, very easy life. I'm very happy and very contented.

(TRANSCRIBED AND EDITED BY TONY STAVEACRE, FROM A CONVERSATION RECORDED IN JUNE 1998)

Historical footnote:

Flo mentioned her mother's maiden name was Deare. William Sampson had lodged with Flo's grandparent's who ran a lodging house in Green Lane Cottage Butcombe.

In Green Lane, Butcombe in the 1901 census:

Name	Rel. to Head of family	Age	Occ.	Place of birth
Robert Deare	Head	62	General Labourer	Bridgewater, Somerset
Mahala Deare	Wife	54		Nempnett, Somerset
George H Mickberdwright	Lodger	33	Stone Mason	Montecute, Somerset
John Marks	Lodger	44	Stone Mason	Nempnett, Somerset

Looking at the previous census in 1891, Robert Deare and his family were living in Salford, near Manchester, possibly working on the Manchester/Liverpool Shipping canal which was completed in 1893.

Extract from the 1891 census, Salford:

Name	Rel. to Head of family	Age	Occ.	Place of birth
Robert Deare	Head	51	General Labourer	Bridgewater, Somerset
Mahala Deare	Wife	45		Nempnett, Somerset
Harry Deare	Son	17	General Labourer	Nempnett, Somerset
James Brown	Boarder	30	General Labourer	Felton, Windford, Somerset

Flo mentioned her father was a Devon man and he walked from Devon to work on the lake. Thurza [Thirza] Victoria and William Sampson were married in 1895.

Extract from the 1901 census, Blagdon:

Name	Rel. to Head of family	Age	Occ.	Place of birth
William Sampson	Head	28	Navvy	Kingsbridge, Devon
Thurza Sampson	Wife	29		Nempnett, Somerset
Harry Sampson	Son	5		Butcombe, Somerset
Edward Sampson	Son	4		Butcombe, Somerset
Robert W Sampson	Son	1		Butcombe, Somerset

At the beginning of the interview Flo mentioned one of her brothers was killed by a horse – the death of Harry Sampson aged 6 is registered in the parish register for September 1901.

From the Blagdon Baptism records:

Baptized on March 23, 1902
January 24, 1902, Edith - parents: William & Thirza Victoria Sampson

The following were all baptized on June 2, 1918, parents William & Thurza Victoria Sampson.

Date of birth	Name
May 1, 1903	*Sidney Albert*
August 3, 1904	*Thurza Anna*
September 10, 1905	*Andrew Jack*
June 21, 1908	*Victoria Bertha*
August 3, 1909	*Richard Cecil*
February 21, 1911	*David Lloyd George*
August 23, 1912	*Mary Florence Eleanor*

Both Flo's parents died at the age of 56, Thirza Victoria in June 1928 and William in February 1931. Flo was convinced that the same fate would befall her in her 56th year but happily she was to live for many more years.

Notes compiled by Sheila Johnson

IKIE SMART
1914–2002

Tony Staveacre

'Me father was more or less a navvie. He had a stall on Bristol market as well, selling fruit and vegetables. He took that on from his mother. We lived in Bishop Sutton then, before we come to Harptree. We lived in a farm cottage. There were five of us children then, and father had the cottage on condition that he worked on the farm. But he wanted his Saturdays off, so that he could go on going to the market. Well that went on for quite some time, and then the farmer said 'I want you all the time.' Father didn't want to give up this job on the market in Bristol, he said he wouldn't do it. So he lost the job, and we were put out on the side of the road, all of the family, with our few bits of furniture and all. That's what the farmers could do in those days. Just because he wouldn't work weekends. I won't say no names, but that farmer, he lives at Harptree still, or his son does anyway. So, we were left standing on the side of the road, and if it hadn't been for another old farmer there, who gave us a little place to go in for a while, we should have been left standing there, with nowhere to go. That's how it was in them days. There were five of us children then, and when we come up to West Harptree there were five more, ten altogether, seven girls and three boys.

We lived right next to the bakery in Harptree, opposite where the garage is now, where you go round the bend to Bishop Sutton. Me father had a big garden, about half an acre, and he grew a lot of stuff for the market, and for to feed the lot of us. He needed a lot of stuff, didn't he? And later on, after the war, he had a horse and cart, and he used to tender for these jobs on the council. Can you remember those old steam rollers? He used to tender for this job, which was to take the water to the steam rollers: he would spray the road in front of the steam roller, and he would get about nine shillings a day for that — horse, man and cart. That went on for a while, till the steam engines went out, and then he went on to work for the electric people, taking the cables out to the hills and that. He'd help them dig the holes to put the posts in. He only had the one horse, an old army horse, finished up from the army. He had a cart, and he also had an old four-wheel wagon, and he'd take a load of people into Weston for an outing in that. It'd hold about ten, I think.

We kids had no choice of what we were going to do in those days. When you left school, the first job that came along — you had to take it. There was no chance of being apprenticed to anyone because you couldn't afford it. You had to take what were coming. In 1928, when I did leave school, farmers used to come in to the schools, and anyone that was leaving school at the Easter holiday — if they were suitable they'd take them on.

That's how I come to go on a farm. Down where the Chew Valley Lake is now. Walk down there at 6 o'clock in the morning, be there till 5 o'clock at night. Seven days a week. I'd be doing any old cagnagging, pulling roots, grinding roots, milking by hand, anything that were going. Chew Park Farm, that was. And that's where I went for the first eight months of my working life. I left school at 14, went straight to work in the Easter holidays. And I've never let up since!

The first I knew about the Mendips, was with the chap that used to drive the grocery van from Harptree. I used to go over the Mendips with him, help him with the deliveries. That was in the days when he had an old lorry with solid tyres. We used to go out across the Mendips to the rifle range. And all along there which is now grass ground, nice grass ground — well, that used to be covered with heather and furze in them days. And I've known us get up there and get stuck in the snow, and we had to carry all the stuff across the fields to the farms. Going back to the 1930s, I suppose that was.

Then there were some timber fellers up at Charterhouse, out at Long Wood. And the chap what was doing it was a friend of my father's, he used to come in our home. And he said one time, 'I do hear Farmer Parker do want somebody along up there, and you'd better go up and see him.' So me and me elder brother went up there. He were on another little farm and he wanted a change. Well, really and truly, he did want more money, 'cos 5 shillings a week weren't much, were it? So we both went up and got to the gate and tossed a coin for who should go in! And I won so I had to go in. I knocked on the door and the old farmer came out with his lantern in his hand — 'Well, come on in', and we had a chat. And then he came down on that Sunday morning to make the arrangements with my father, then he came back again on the next Sunday, and said he wanted the both of us. And that's how we both came to be up there at Swymmer's Farm, right at the top of Two Trees. We lived in. Did that for four years till I got married, then I managed to get this little place to live in, but I still went on working there, for another seventeen years. My first wage at Chew Park was five shillings a week and three meals a day. At Swymmer's Farm it was twelve shillings and sixpence a week, living in. I'd take my washing home for mother to wash, give her a shilling a week for washing, and so we had eleven shillings a week to spend, and to save. That went on until I was getting a pound a week just before I got married. Then the agreement was that when I got married I should get two pound a week. And that were to keep a home going and all. And most people were only getting that kind of money in them days. Farm labourers, and that sort of outdoor work.

I always enjoyed my work. 'Twere hard, mind. I mean, you go out picking roots in the field when there's snow on the ground, and the tops of the swedes are covered in ice and you had to knock it off with a stick to get them out of the ground. That sort of work were hard, weren't it? And if you had to get up on a rick in the middle of a field, and take the thatch off, and start cutting and hauling the hay into the farm. There were none of these bales then, 'twere all loose mows, you cut it out with a hay knife. We worked from 6 o'clock till 5.30, and in the summer so long as it was light, for the hay-making and that.

I learned how to lay a hedge on me own. I used to go to the competitions and watch others doing it. I picked it up gradually. There's no trick to hedging, you just learn it as you go along, and improve on it. You can make a hedge out of anything, if you know how to do it — thorn, nut-hazel, anything. You just lay it down, stake it on, and make a nice fence. In the end I could beat the lot. I've got all they cups to prove it. And I had prizes for thatching as well, and for sheep-shearing. I done a lot of different things. We do still have a few competitions for hedging now, and I give lessons every spring.

There was no machinery on the farm back in them days. You had to drive a horse in a plough. I used to have a team of three horses one time. Three in line abreast, except if you were pulling a binder, you'd have a trace horse then. But if the three horses were in line abreast, you'd have what they called a three-horse Watkin, two on one side and one on the other and that would balance up the thing – two on the short side and one on the other, and that did balance it nicely. I loved horses. I used to ride a bit one time. Not hunting or anything like that. But just a bit of riding, there's lots of nice places to ride up here. And break 'em in, we used to do that. Farmer Parker used to hunt. His father had a chestnut and in the summertime, he used to say to me, 'Ride the chestnut down home to dinner, to save you pushing the bicycle back up the hill!', and I used to love riding him down. And there's an old chestnut tree out back there where I did tie him up. And going back up one day, when I got to that grass verge up by Frank Watts's place I did let 'im go and away he went, and he stumbled on one of they ditches, and over he went and off I came. The horse was already back in his stable when I got up there! I don't suppose I'd have ever given up the horses, only when the tractors come in and my son was growing up, I said, well I have to move on so I did. I bought my first tractor then. It's still out there, in the garage.

Then I went on timber felling for some years, cutting down trees and things like that. We've hauled fern: we used to haul a lot of fern off Black Down, making ricks with it for bedding. At this end where it's steep we'd cut it with a scythe. On the bit that's more level, you could get up there with a mowing machine. Black Down is nearly 1000 feet above sea level. When you get a blizzard up there, you could have cattle buried in the snow, which we have had. With only their heads showing. 'Tis rough up there, mind.

Up Priddy Hill once, I can remember, the snow was so deep you could stand on the top of it and reach the telephone wires. When it used to be really bad, we'd have snow on Boxing Day and it have kept on till April. Of course, we couldn't do anything then, we had to work on the roads, clearing the snow.

You have a good view of the sea from here, and we used to say, 'If you can see the sea quite plain, then it's likely to rain' – so the rain is very close. If 'twas hazy, then it's going to be fine weather. That's what we used to say anyway. They reckon that the first rain after Priddy Fair is winter rain! But I shouldn't think that's hardly right. We've had some nice weather in September, haven't we, before now.

Priddy Fair has changed a lot. In the old days there were none of them amusements. Then it were all sheep and cattle, and they had a big pen for ponies. A lot of ponies do still come now. And there was a pen for cattle, but they don't have the cattle now. But they didn't have roundabouts and things in them days, it was just the farmers, a sheep fair. We had a fair down here at Ubley too. I'd drive the sheep down to Ubley.

There was also Farringdon Market and Winford Market, that's where the farmers did generally go to sell their stock. In them days there weren't many cattle or sheep fat on Mendip. They used to bring them up to the 'store' stage, then the under-the-hill farmers would buy them and finish them off. Get them fat on the better land. Priddy Fair were out for the store cattle or sheep. Or the fresh lot of ewes.

Of course, they used to reckon in them days that around about Priddy Fair, the farmers had to get rid of some stock to pay their rent! 'Cos rent day did come on about the 29th of September and that's when they did have the Fair.

Priddy is a nice areal for to visit nowadays, isn't it? And have a drink and a meal. Another chap and me did once have a paper round up at Priddy. They did bring the *Evening World* to the Wellsway Inn, and we did take them on from there round Priddy, and 'twas a penny a paper, and we did get threepence a dozen delivering them. Saturday paper was supposed to be tuppence. That was for delivering them the rest of the week. But you couldn't get that penny out of the farmers! Then we'd go into the Hunters Lodge and get a half a pint of beer, and that was all our delivery money gone! That only went on a little while. We thought we were going to make our fortune!

The big difference today from then, is that there used to be a lot of small farms. They might have just a few cattle, 20 or 30 milkers, and the milk would be picked up at the gate, wouldn't it? It all changed when these big milk tankers came along, then they paid the small farmers to get rid of their cows, and to stick with the big farms. But what I used to call a farmer in the old days, he had a few cows, he had a few sheep, he had a few pigs and hens and that sort of thing. But you call them farmers now, they'm only milk producers or beef producers or corn producers. Old farmers did always grow a bit of corn and keep some of everything. In the old days they were more or less self-supporting.

I only kept sheep in later years, 'cos I didn't have the facilities in the old days. How I come to have the first bit of land was in the time when I used to help all the hill farmers with a bit of hedging and thatching. One lady I did do a bit of work for, Miss Watts, where Joe Cryer is now, she did own land at Ubley Drove, and she let me the land when it become vacant, and that's where I started keeping a few cattle and sheep. Then I got a bit more, a bit at a time. I used to rent all the land over there on the other side of Rhodyate at one time. I always liked the sheep. 'Tis more convenient than anything else. It's easier to get a bit of money out of them, I suppose. And 'tis nice to see sheep when they've just got their lambs. It's nice to see the lambs playing about when they'm young.

Farmers were more friendly in the old days than what they are now. I've seen one farmer hay-making in a field, and another farmer is going by in his horse and cart, and he had nothing to do himself – so he'd be in there helping! And you'd never go by a field, and see a man working there without stopping to have a chat with him. But now they all go tearing by, and never know you'm there, do they? Yes, they were very friendly in the old days. But there was nothing much else a farmer could do than to be friendly, were there? Except that they'd meet at market, they didn't see anybody else. There was nothing farmers would like more than to visit one another – 'you come and see my cattle or my corn' - you know, appraise it for one another. But now they wouldn't bother, would 'em? Everything's different now, isn't it? You've got to be more educated, and keep more books and that. In the old days you didn't bother. You'ld sell to the next farmer or you'ld buy at market. Book-keeping was quite simple in the old days.

Today, you couldn't sell milk from the door, or sell vegetables. Well, maybe you could on the quiet! In them days you could do what you liked. But today you have to do everything by the book, and fill in forms, haven't you? Even the cattle and sheep now – if you want this subsidy, you have to register them to get it, which I think 'tis unnecessary. 'Tis spending public money where there's no need of it, I think.

In the war, we were in what they called a Reserved Occupation on the farm. We were also in the Rescue Service – the ARP. We were called out to Weston in the bombing raids, and helped to get people out from houses that had been bombed. Otherwise we carried on with farming all the same. But it was hard on the farmers. There were two of us up there working, and both of us were in the ARP. And they had us down to Weston for two or three nights, and the farmer had to do all the milking hisself. Well, that didn't go down very well! They wouldn't let us go home, 'cos we were still getting people out who were buried, weren't we? They dropped some of them Molotov Cocktails over the other side of the hill, and that were a sight to behold. Incendiaries. The school here got some of those in the roof, but they put the fire out quickly. Everybody got incendiaries in their garden. Then we would pick up the night fighters' shells, which they would drop as they did go over. I found some up on the plough grounds where we were working. They were in belts.

They made a fake airport up on Black Down, they made like flare paths, as though it was an aerodrome. But they only had about two bombs dropped up there. And the Air Force personnel were billeted in the farms. Then they had a sudden ideal that the Germans might try and land gliders up there, and we had gangs going up there on a Sunday morning to put up those great mounds, to stop the gliders landing. They even had big barges on the lake, to stop flying boats landing on there, with oil drums and that.

There was quite a bit of black market going on in the war. But I mustn't say too much about that, 'twouldn't do! Some farmers from the Mendips went to gaol over that. And there were a bit of fiddling with the petrol coupons. If you had a petrol engine you could get coupons for the fuel, and you could put in for some more, if you did want to cut some chaff or summat. And they'd give you some coupons for that. If you didn't use the petrol all for that, you could use it for something else. But it were up to everybody to get what they could, I suppose. I kept some pigs up here one time, a couple of big baconers. And I had some friends would come out from town for a bit of bacon, mind. A nice ham or summat like that. Same with the farmers – if they did kill a sheep or a pig, a nice side of bacon would go down very well, wouldn't it, for anyone that could afford to buy it! You had to get a licence, once a year, for to kill a pig for yourself. And some did get a licence and kill about three! They had what they called the Small Pig Breeders Association. And you did bring up the pig, and when they did need them for to kill, they did take them off you. It was like a club. And the last lot I had, I had 20 baconers ready in the barn up there, and they didn't want 'em! What was I to do? I'm feeding them and feeding them, and they just didn't want 'em at that time. So that didn't pay.

I've done everything on a farm in my life. I've got ten acres up there, I've grown wheat and I've grown potatoes. But not in a big way, only for myself, like. Now I've got half a dozen cattle and I've thirty sheep, and that's enough for me. The sheep were at Ubley until this morning, now I've brought them down to that field behind where the hairdresser's shop is. I've had the run of that ground for years. In the old days, when you moved your stock, you'd drive them along the roads. I remember a chap at Dundry bought a cow and a calf off of Parker, and I drove them from there to the Blue Bowl down at Harptree, and then his chap come and pick them up from there, and drove them up to Dundry. That's how things used to be done like that. You had drovers that would take on those jobs, to drive cattle – some times on long distances. One old man used to bring his stallion round to all the farms, on a lead!

When I come to Blagdon first, most of the villagers were down this road – all these little cottages on Rhodyate were owned by villagers and we knew them all. I've heard tell that when they had the lead miners working up at Charterhouse, that was when a lot of these cottages in Blagdon were built, what they call 'sundowner' cottages. If they could build four walls up and a hearth, and get a fire going by sundown, they could claim the ground that they were standing on then. In fact I think Eve's grandfather did work up there at Charterhouse, William Day, who owned this house before we came here.

But then when they built the council houses over there on the Bath Road, the villagers got tired of these little places, and wanted something more modern. And townies then came and bought these cottages and did do them up. And so me and Mavis are really the only ones left now from them days, the others are all gone.

Local artist Martin Bentham with Ikie Smart and George Symes
Photo: Derek Maybee.

I only once ever thought of leaving here, and going somewhere else. And I might have went. A friend of mine and me, we were both working up on Mendip then and living in, and at that time, his brother went to Canada! on that assisted passage thing, and he'd done very well there. You could get so many acres to clear, and the government would help you with it. And if you did get on with that, then you could get some more. And so we made up our minds to do it. But when we went in to see them about it, they'd stopped it! And we couldn't afford to pay for it on our own, of course, so we had to give it up and stay around here. That was in the 1930s. I wasn't married then. But then of course, when you get married, you have to forget all they things, and get on with your life, don't you …?!'

(Transcribed and edited by Tony Staveacre, from a conversation recorded in September 1993)

Historical footnote:

Ikie Smart mentioned his father running a fruit and vegetable stall in Bristol market, a business he'd taken over from his mother.

In the 1901 census in Upper Sutton, Chew Magna:

Name	Rel. to Head	Age	Occupation	Place of birth
Harriet Smart	Head	58	Market Gardener	Chew Magna
Isaac Smart	Son	20	General labourer	Chew Stoke
Emily Smart	Daur.	16		Chew Stoke
William Easton	Boarder	20	General labourer	Monmouth

Ikie Smart's father is 20 years old, living with his widowed mother, a market gardener.

In the 1891 census, 2 Wick's Green, Bishop Sutton:

Name	Rel. to Head	Age	Occupation	Place of birth
Harriet Smart	Head	39?	Market Gardener	Chew Magna
Stephen Smart	Son	20		Chew Stoke
Isaac Smart	Son	10		Chew Stoke
Emily Smart	Daur.	7		Chew Stoke

In 1881 Isaac's grandfather, another Isaac, was still alive and the family were living in Providence Place, Chew Stoke

Name	Rel. to Head	Age	Occupation	Place of birth
Isaac Smart	Head	34	Agricultural Labourer	Chew Stoke
Harriet Smart	Wife	36		Chew Magna
Daniel Smart	Son	11	Scholar	Chew Stoke
Stephen Smart	Son	9	Scholar	Chew Stoke
Isaac Smart	Son	1		Chew Stoke

Looking back to 1851, Isaac's grandfather was the son of Daniel and Nancy Smart. Daniel Smart was a *'freeholder and farmer of 178 acres employing 3 labs.* [labourers], *besides sons'* in Chew Stoke.

Name	Rel. to Head	Age	Occupation	Place of birth
Daniel Smart	Head	54	Farmer	Winford
Nancy -ditto-	Wife	45		Wrington
John -ditto-	Son	19		Chew Stoke
James −ditto-	Son	17		Chew Stoke
Stephen −ditto-	Son	13		Chew Stoke
Isaac −ditto-	Son	6		Chew Stoke
Elizabeth −ditto-	Daur.	16		Chew Stoke
Emina −ditto-	Daur.	10		Chew Stoke
Hannah −ditto-	Daur.	8mths		Chew Stoke
Leah Walker		22	House Servant	East Harptree
William Haskins		32	Farm Servant	Chew Stoke

Nancy was a widow by 1861, John and James had left home and the farm had shrunk to 150 acres – Nancy died in 1865. From the census in 1871, the sons were married and mostly working as agricultural labourers, the farm seems to have been sold off.

Notes compiled by Sheila Johnson

LECTURE TOPICS AND OPEN FORUM MEETINGS
HELD DURING 2005 AND 2006

January	Lecture - The Wrington Vale Light Railway Colin Maggs MBE, MA
February	Forum – C20th Healthcare in Blagdon (part 1)
February	Lecture - Windmills and millers in Somerset (and AGM) Sarah Harris
March	Lecture - The Victoria County History of Somerset Dr. Robert Dunning
March	Forum – C20th Healthcare in Blagdon (part 2)
April	Lecture - History of stereo photography – Alan Gray
April	Visit by Somerset Vernacular Building Research Group John Dallimore et al.
May	Lecture - Bells and bellringers – Michael Horseman
June	The Portable Antiquities Scheme - Kurt Adams – deferred
July	Local potteries – Vince Russett – ditto
August	Forum – My ancestors in Blagdon: the Balls and the Lyons Helen Williams (Australia)
September	Lecture - The Romans in and around Blagdon Siobhan Watson MA
October	Forum - A Blagdon childhood remembered – Mary Hibberd
November	Lecture - Victorian servants - Pat Hase MA

Lecture and forum topics 2006

January	Forum - Recreation & Leisure in Blagdon
February	Lecture - Somerset Record Office, Esther Ormerod (and AGM)
February	Forum – Recreation & Leisure in Blagdon (part 2)
March	Forum - Blagdon businesses and employment
April	Lecture - The life of agricultural labourers in C18, Dr Alan Dodge
May	Forum - Blagdon Fire Service
June	Lecture - Anarchy of King Stephen in Bristol & East Harptree William Evans
July	Lecture - Farm buildings: vanishing heritage, Linda Hall
September	Lecture - Mills, Coal, and Glass in Stanton Drew, Colin Budge
October	Forum - Blagdon's Water Supply
November	Lecture - Cheddar cheese and Frome Cheese Show (archive films) Brian Haynes

Note – Forum meetings = *C20th Village History Forum*

All the past Recent History Group notes are being written up for deposit into the Society's archives and will provide primary source material for research and future essays that will form the records of life during the 20th century in Blagdon. In addition to the notes are CDs and tapes of recordings of present and past village residents' memories and experiences that together will make a significant and unique archive of life in this Mendip village. Hopefully these records will provide the inspiration for future historians to write and publish future volumes in the ever developing *History of Blagdon*.

Olga Shotton and Neil Bentham

Appendix B

The topics listed below are awaiting the interest of willing researchers. Those marked ★ are being actively researched.

The geology of the local area
Studies in the history of some of Blagdon's older houses★
The growth and development of Blagdon★
Population growth and occupations in Blagdon★
Food, cider and orchards
Lords of the Manor
Field names★
The Roman Church before the Reformation★
The Parish Church of St. Andrew★
The Methodist Church★
The Baptist Church★
The Cemetery
Old Coombe Lodge★
The effect of WW1 and WW2 on Blagdon
Local Businesses★
Turnpikes and Transport
Bristol Waterworks and drainage
Electrical, Gas and Telephone services to Blagdon
Famous People associated with Blagdon★
Hannah More – Part Two★
Births, Marriages, Deaths and Families
The Normans and Domesday
Blagdon and the New Poor Law 1834★
Postal Services
Police Services
Fire Services
Sports and pastimes
The Rev. Augustus Montague Toplady★
Newspapers and the Press

The Society would be pleased to receive articles, photographs and memorabilia from the community and particularly offers to undertake the basic research on any of the topics listed above – some already have been the subject of a Recent History Group Forum and any other topic or aspects of the village of interest.